YOU'RE NEXT!

YOU'RE NEXT!

How one company changed the way we shop

TERRY GREEN

Marshall Cavendish
Business

Copyright © 2011 Terence Green
First published in 2011 by Marshall Cavendish Business
An imprint of Marshall Cavendish International

PO Box 65829
London EC1P 1NY
United Kingdom
info@marshallcavendish.co.uk

and

1 New Industrial Road
Singapore 536196
genrefsales@sg.marshallcavendish.com
www.marshallcavendish.com/genref

Marshall Cavendish is a trademark of Times Publishing Limited

Other Marshall Cavendish offices:
Marshall Cavendish International (Asia) Private Limited, 1 New Industrial Road, Singapore 536196 •
Marshall Cavendish Corporation. 99 White Plains Road, Tarrytown NY 10591–9001, USA • Marshall
Cavendish International (Thailand) Co Ltd. 253 Asoke, 12th Floor, Sukhumvit 21 Road, Klongtoey
Nua, Wattana, Bangkok 10110, Thailand • Marshall Cavendish (Malaysia) Sdn Bhd, Times Subang,
Lot 46, Subang Hi-Tech Industrial Park, Batu Tiga, 40000 Shah Alam, Selangor Darul Ehsan, Malaysia

The right of Terence Green to be identified as the authors of this work has been asserted by them in
accordance with the Copyright, Designs and Patents Act 1988.

A CIP record for this book is available from the British Library

ISBN 978-981-4302-61-6

Cover design by Staziker Jones
Printed and bound in the United Kingdom by TJ International

I dedicate this book to innovators everywhere.
Innovation – the successful exploitation of new ideas – is at the
heart of every great enterprise. May this story give you
the courage to back your own ideas and inspire you
to new heights of creativity and success.

CONTENTS

PREFACE

I QUEUE THEREFORE I AM

So here I am standing, glass of wine in hand, at yet another social occasion, when someone I've just met asks the inevitable question.

"So, what do you do for a living?"

Deep breath, and away we go. "Picture yourself standing in line at the post office." Pause. "Waiting to be served." Pause again. "When the clerk is ready to see you, he presses a button, and a voice sounds out, 'Cashier Number Three Please.' – Well, that's me. That's my voice."

"No!" Hushed tones. "I always thought that was Roger Moore! That's amazing. Go on – say it again!"

"Cashier Number Nineteeeen, please! – Yes, I do all of the other numbers as well, but only in the male voice you understand."

"It really is you, isn't it?"

So starts another conversation about queueing. Everyone I meet has been there – supermarkets, hospitals, airports, government offices, even favourite coffee shops – all contribute to our rich experiences of badly managed queues.

Sometimes I hear the most outrageous anecdotes – and I tuck them all away for my virtual scrapbook of queueing stories. Here's one...

"It was Christmas and I had taken the kids to Santa's Grotto at the big toy store in town. The line was really long. It took over an hour to get near the front, but my two were so excited that they didn't mind. Just as we were about to get inside the grotto, this posh-looking man arrived trailing a five-year-old. He took one look at the queue, stuck his nose firmly in the air, and pushed in ahead of us. The lady in front of us lost it completely. She started attacking him with her umbrella, and calling him all the names under the sun. Two elves came over to calm things down. A tussle broke out. One of them grabbed the man's arm, and he tripped. Pretty soon he was flat on the floor, with this elf astride him giving him what for. I hadn't laughed so much in ages!"

WHEN I WAS A STUDENT, I signed up for a foundation course in marketing because I overheard the lecturer say, "Marketing is the most fun you can have with your clothes on." He was, of course, exaggerating. But he was good – could have sold tuxedoes to penguins – and his course captured my imagination. I learned that to create a sustainable business, you must give customers a compelling reason to keep coming back for more. Our first customer for "Cashier Number Three Please," the UK Post Office, is still a major customer today, over fifteen years later – a fact of which I am very proud.

Twenty years ago queue management was hardly ever mentioned. Today that's changed dramatically. Many organisations in the UK and the USA now talk about service issues, and put senior executives in charge of customer experience. I would like to think that my colleagues and I have contributed to that change in some small way.

I am being too modest. We have made a huge difference. These days the company I helped to found, Qm, is part of a global enterprise called

Qmatic, which has around 50,000 systems in use in 110 countries across the world. A number equivalent to about a quarter of the world's population benefit from better, faster service every year as a result.

But there is still a long way to go. I estimate that over £2 billion and 2,000 years of people's time are still wasted every year through badly managed queues. And that's just in the UK. This state of affairs is repeated everywhere in the world. What a cost to society! It's time to change it for the better, to eliminate queueing waste, to save money and to give back to people their precious time.

Terry Green
September 2010

01

INTRODUCTION

I took a deep breath. As I rode the elevator skywards, I tried to marshall my thoughts. Twelve floors of shiny stainless steel and glass passed me by. It had taken six months of emails, phone calls, and patient, polite follow-ups to get this meeting. There was too much at stake to fail now. The lady I was about to meet, a senior executive of a major bank, had a reputation for taking no prisoners. I had heard that her meetings rarely lasted longer than 20 minutes before terrified salesmen were sent scurrying back to the lift. I would have to work fast if I wanted a fair hearing today. I had to grab them in the critical first 90 seconds of the meeting – or all would be lost. I was ready.

Inside the office, pleasantries over, I took another deep breath. "It's about valuing time," I began. "It's about matching your customer's need for service with the best available staff in the most efficient way. In the last fifteen years I have worked with three of the UK's leading banks and 15 of the top 25 retailers, and we have produced some astounding results. Lower operating costs, richer customer experiences, greater customer loyalty and ultimately, increased sales. We can help you."

Silence. As all good salesmen will tell you, at this point it was vital to remain quiet and let my customer speak. Their next words tell you whether you are heading towards an order – or the door. The seconds ticked by.

2

"So who else have you done this for?" she asked. "Give me an example."

We were off. In a few sentences I told her how I had worked with Argos, a major UK retailer, and how the system we implemented not only boosted customer satisfaction but also maximised valuable store space and staff hours. She was listening. In the next 45 minutes we talked about the nature of queueing, and why you can't just wish it away, the impact on

IT'S ABOUT VALUING TIME. It's about matching your customer's need for service with the best available staff in the most efficient way.

waiting customers' psyches and propensity to buy, and the real financial benefits of doing it right. She was hooked. I didn't use a single Powerpoint slide – just pen and paper.

As we walked back to the lift after the meeting, she turned to me. "It's a great pleasure to meet someone who is so passionate about what they do," she said. "I look forward to working with you."

I'M IN THE QUEUEING BUSINESS and, as you know by now, I am the voice of "Cashier Number Three Please" in around 8,500 locations across the UK – in retailers, banks, railway stations, all manner of places – helping the public get served faster. But that's only part of the story.

In 2004 our company, Qm Group was sold to our management team, who were backed by venture capitalists, Advantage Capital, and I stayed on to help out. In 2007 we sold again, and this time to Swedish venture capitalists, Altor Equity Partners, who also bought Qmatic, a Swedish rival of ours. I now sit on the board of the combined Qmatic Group as a non-executive director.

I don't claim to have invented our systems – other, much more talented colleagues devised the technical solutions. I sell ideas. That's my thing. My role has been to convince client organisations of the importance of queueing within their business model, and then to work with them to optimise the benefits.

Unplanned and unmanaged queues are waste. They waste customers' time, they waste staff hours, and they waste sales floor space. Yes, everyone expects to queue, but that doesn't stop them resenting an exploitation of their valuable time. Yet retailers are reluctant to plan for queues; it feels like failure to even admit the possibility.

It doesn't have to be this way. Every retailer or bank I have worked with has been able to define a course of action which improved things and saved money. Not everyone has taken my advice, but that's their choice. The ones who did have not regretted it.

I've come to be, over the last 15 years, something of a Queue Guru. I have sat in countless boardrooms, worked alongside warehouse staff, posed as a mystery shopper; I have walked shopping malls, interviewing consumers about their favourite stores; I have presented to halls full of bankers at conferences; I have manned exhibition stands preaching to retailers the good words, "queue" and "management."

My opinions are based not only on my years of experience as a supplier but also as an inveterate shopper. I like to shop. (Ask anyone who knows me about my shirt collection.) Shopping of any kind – even supermarket shopping – can be a rich experience. Smells, textures, colours and sound influence the way we feel about the trip that we make, and help to transform a potentially boring necessity into an adventure.

To get our attention, retailers compete to give us the latest products, at the best prices, in the smartest stores. Yet all too often they leave to chance the one thing that makes an immeasurable difference: Service. All stores have staff available to assist shoppers; but it is the way they organise the provision of service that makes a difference. This is the difference between increased sales and lost customers. Attempting to reduce the cost of each transaction might produce savings in the short term but runs the risk of driving customers away if service levels are eroded. Conversely, an initiative to serve customers faster can drive up staff cost and drive down service levels.

I LIKE TO SHOP. Ask anyone who knows me about my shirt collection.

In the world of queue management, things are not always what they seem.

02

SHOPPING
FOR BUSINESS

ARE WE BEING SERVED?

In 2003 I carried out a speculative project for a UK-based electricals retail chain who were curious about how we could help them improve the customer experience in their stores. So I spent a day in one of their edge-of-town outlets in Oxford – a busy Saturday – to watch how it worked.

The store was around 50,000 square feet, with departments for all of the major electrical items – flat-screen TVs, home cinema, white goods, personal computers, digital cameras. The store had an FTE of eight, which means a "full-time equivalent" staffing level of just eight people for such a huge space.

I watched customers arrive at the store. Typically they first looked around and then moved into the area that interested them. There they would start to examine the individual items, flitting from one product to the next. The fun began when they settled, like tired butterflies, onto a particular product of interest. They would read the label several times over, looking for the hidden meaning behind the few short lines of small, cryptic text. They would stand back and look at neighbouring products, playing "spot the difference": Which TV would look better in the sitting room? How come this one costs so much more than that one? Sooner or later the customers who had a serious interest would decide that they needed help from a sales person. And here came the challenge: How do you get a salesman to understand that you want their help without attracting attention to yourself?

Shoppers are self-conscious beings, wary in the retailer's territory. Apart from the few who are endowed with high levels of confidence, most just want to get through the whole experience without causing a ripple. (The British, in particular, are a race apart when it comes to trying to send out a covert signal which they hope will be invisible to all except the nearest sales person.)

I noted several techniques in play. Stand on the spot, head thrust up, shoulders back, and look from side to side. Walk around the product of interest in an agitated manner, covering the same piece of floor time and again like a tiger prowling around his cage. Stand motionless looking into space, preferably with a hand placed possessively on the item of desire. Sometimes when a free salesman was spotted

> **HOW DO YOU GET a salesman to understand that you want their help, without attracting attention to yourself?**

on the far side of the store, a hot pursuit began, the shopper making a mad dash for the salesman before anyone else could get hold of him. Those who shopped in pairs had an advantage – one member could wait by the product and do the territorial dance, while another charged around the showroom floor tackling anyone who looked like a salesman.

I looked around the store. All of the key departments were arranged around its edge, while the space in the centre was filled with rows of kettles, irons, phones and other relatively low-value items. As I watched I realised that all of the unoccupied staff were prowling around the edges.

Were they frightened of open spaces? Agoraphobia seemed like a weird trait to look for in your sales team. I asked the manager.

"Ah," he said, "the sales people are discouraged from helping customers in that area."

Interesting, I thought. "Why?"

"All the items there are low-priced. We don't make enough money on them to justify a sales person helping."

I was intrigued. "But surely if you give great service to a customer for a kettle today, he will be more likely to buy his next TV from you?"

"It's head office policy, I'm afraid."

We were standing amongst the kettles. A thought struck me.

"Why do some of the products in this area have a Best Buy sticker on them? Does that mean they are great value or have the best features? And who decides they are a Best Buy?"

"Oh, that's just a code for the sales guys," said the manager. "The ones with the stickers are where we make the best margin, and so if a salesman is dragged into this area he will always recommend a Best Buy."

This was getting interesting. I could understand why it was important to control staff costs – after all, it's the one big variable cost in running the store – but I couldn't understand how they had arrived at eight staff as the right answer. It seemed to me that they had tried to guess a number by which most of the staff would be occupied most of the time, and hence fewer staff hours wasted. But this must mean that at least some of the time there would be too many customers for all to be comfortably served, leading to stress as well as lost sales.

So this policy would actually limit sales volumes when the store was busy, and hand dissatisfied customers to the competition – not something that was desirable when trying to run a successful business.

What was needed was data not guesses.

Thinking it through, if we could put a system in place that allowed customers to say when they wanted to help, and what level of help they needed, and we could match those requests up with available staff in store, then not only could we manage customer requests better, we would also be able to collect data for fine-tuning future staffing levels to control costs while maximising sales.

This would change the fundamental dynamic of the store – the way customers accessed help and advice. Instead of sales people passively waiting for customers to find them, we could select the sales person who had the best product knowledge to match up with "hot sales requests" collected by the queue management system. Suddenly sales people would have an incentive to improve their knowledge and improve service across the store.

IT'S HEAD OFFICE policy, I'm afraid...

As it was, though, without this incentive, the sales people became passive. The store's strategy was effectively eroding the reasons for shopping there.

The meeting I subsequently had with the director of operations summarised the management's attitude to shoppers very well. She made herself difficult to pin down for a meeting, and the date we finally agreed on was the morning of Christmas Eve. In a spirit of goodwill I took festive mince pies to the meeting. Walking into the Dickensian, decoration-free office was like having an appointment with Scrooge. I expected someone to shout "Humbug!" at any moment. These people clearly took themselves very seriously. I sat in her office a full ten minutes before she showed up.

"As its Christmas Eve I brought you some mince pies," I said, "Merry Christmas!"

No reaction. My festive offering was placed in a desk drawer. It was never mentioned again. No coffee or other refreshment was offered.

I presented my findings from the store visit, and proposed a radical rethink of how to organise staff and allocate service on the shop floor.

My advice fell on deaf ears. They weren't interested. The concepts that I presented were just too alien to the organisation's philosophy.

Well, you can't win them all. The solution that we arrived at for this problem went on to be highly successful elsewhere and is today catching on like wildfire in the retail banking sector – but more of this later.

All retailers are of course subject to the laws of economics. They would quickly go out of business if they had too many staff, hired just in case we decide we need help while shopping. But it's a question of balance and of context.

WHAT MAKES PEOPLE SHOP?

Most consumers now regularly use the internet to access information about products, check prices and, increasingly, make purchases. In this age of 24/7 online shopping, why do shoppers still shop?

1. We want to see and feel an item before we buy it

The store allows us to "test drive" potential purchases before we commit.

Items like clothing fall into this category (although as customers get used to the returns services offered by online vendors this becomes less compelling). In my case I love to browse bookstores, to pick a book up and read the first few pages before I decide if it's for me. For others it might be choosing a PC or a pair of shoes.

2. We want face-to-face contact

We crave the reassurance of talking to someone face to face before we commit – especially when it is a purchase we'll have to live with for a long time, a purchase with big implications for our future wealth, or a purchase where the ongoing service aspect represents a major part of the proposition. The banks see this a lot. Over 70% of all major financial products sold by banks are signed up for face-to-face.

3. Shopping is a leisure experience

We enjoy the thrill of the chase going from store to store, window shopping, flirting with the idea of buying something; while we may not necessarily set out to make a purchase today, with the right cues and persuasion, we might just be seduced.

4. Shopping is a social activity

Friends or family meet up and shop together. It's fun, and it's also a way for the group to explore their collective values, to bond with one another, and to come closer together. This process not only results in spontaneous purchases but also in the setting of "rules" around what an individual will purchase in future.

5. We want instant gratification

If we go online, we can have a product shipped, but at the store we can get it right now.

For all of these reasons, the shopper chooses the store over the online portal. Retailers must recognise that this is the role that their stores now play.

How the store then attends to shoppers therefore becomes crucial. Sales staff must be visible, accessible, and knowledgeable; the checkout process must be smooth and painless. Otherwise, the whole enterprise is undermined. The shopper who has come to the store to see, to feel, to talk, to socialise, walks right back out.

Timely service delivery thus clearly plays a key role in the shopping experience. Confident, articulate sales people who know their products can sell a customer up the range by matching his needs to the available stock more closely. This leads to more satisfied customers and more revenue for the store. Conversely, a badly managed checkout process can leave a bad taste in the shopper's mouth, and ruin all the good work that's gone into the rest of the journey. But perhaps the most crucial part of this process is the waiting.

THE WAITING GAME

Waiting comes between the wanting and the getting. Whenever there is something that you want that can't be had straight away there is a wait and therefore a waiting experience. And if there are more than two people waiting for service there is a queue.

Children don't like waiting for anything, but as we become adults we are socialised into the belief that waiting is a necessary part of life's experience. Not all waiting is unpleasant. Knowing that you have a holiday booked in a few weeks' time – when you will be able to lie on the beach, explore the beautiful coastline, partake of lavish seafood – can bring an anticipatory thrill to the dullest work day. Equally, a well-managed wait in store can give you time to explore the idea of your purchase and assimilate new information which might enhance the pleasure in your purchase.

Some waiting is a necessary part of life – waiting for my laptop to boot up, the traffic lights to change – a host of situations in our everyday lives hold us back from instant gratification of our desires.

Shopping is no exception. In fact, any environment where we need face-to-face service will have situations in which consumers have to wait their turn. The way the waiting is managed has a huge impact on customer experience, sales and cost.

There's a lesson to be learnt here from theme parks. Theme parks are about fun. People go there to experience the thrill of the attractions. And yet how much of the day is spent on the actual rides? Probably no more than 30%. The rest of the time is spent moving between rides, taking refreshment breaks, and queueing for the next ride.

Theme parks have thus become the stars of the waiting game – and Disney indisputably the masters. Their work on managing the perception of waiting customers has been an integral part of the success of their parks. Lines for rides are managed so that they move continuously and smoothly. Signs announcing expected waiting times are displayed prominently. Staff in costume entertain the waiting crowds and make the queue feel like its part of the adventure.

On top of that, Disney realised that visitors who are waiting in line are missing out on other attractions and not spending money. The Fast-Pass™ scheme was thus introduced, to give visitors the choice between standing in line for a particular ride or pre-booking a future slot. Future slots are valid for a one hour window giving visitors some flexibility for the exact time that they return. Being able to wait "virtually" means that visitors now participate in more revenue-generating activities within the park, and can take more rides instead of being held up in a queue. This has led to a significant increase in customer satisfaction.[1]

> THEME PARKS are about fun. But how much of the day is spent on the actual rides?

When our waiting time is managed well, it ceases to be an issue to us. It becomes just another part of the day's experience and not one on which we consumers dwell.

Theme parks know this. But do other businesses? Their responses vary from complete indifference to genuine efforts to improve things. This spectrum of attitudes is reflected in the quality and timeliness of the service that we as consumers receive – not just in retail stores but in all situations – between the wanting and the getting.

In the last 20 years many organisations have made major strides to improve the quality of service that they deliver in their stores. For me, working in the UK, it all started with the Post Office, the place where my voice first became famous.

03

POST EARLY FOR
SUCCESS

EARLY DAYS

In the early 1990s, the Post Office decided to tackle the long-standing issue of perceived waiting time within their branches. In the old set-up a line would form at each open window. Arriving customers would determine which queue to join by trying to guess which one would move fastest. Simple right? Just join the line with the fewest people in it. Wrong.

Once we understood the range of activities that customers might undertake when they got to the counter – buying some stamps might take two minutes, whereas getting a passport checked might take 20 – we realised just how wrong an assumption this was. As a customer joining a line, your waiting time would be the sum of the service times of the people in front of you. Without knowing their planned tasks, it was impossible to predict your waiting time reliably.

Imagine the frustration when on joining the shortest line, the long line next to you moves much faster and you realize that you joined the wrong queue? Should you switch lines – and if you do, will that line suddenly slow down and the one that you left suddenly move forward? Invariably!

There is nothing quite as frustrating as being a time-pressed shopper standing in a line and watching the lines on either side of you get served faster. It raises your stress level and makes you more conscious of the passing seconds. Anything which in normal circumstances might have been a minor irritation becomes a major issue.

Multiple lines might be mathematically the most efficient way of getting customers served but they expose the customer to huge and unpredictable variations in waiting time, making the shopper feel like a helpless victim of the system. Mathematical efficiency isn't the only criteria to use when determining how best to manage people's wait.

It's surprising then, that a whole category of retail stores still believes that this is the way to get things done. I am talking about supermarkets. And the weekly misery they subject their shoppers to as the massed ranks of shopping carts descend on the checkouts. They might have coping strategies that try to match the number of staff to demand at peak times, but fundamentally the way that they organise payment is wrong.

MOVING TO LINEAR QUEUES

Meanwhile back at the Post Office, a new queueing concept was becoming a reality: Linear queues. In the first instance the Post Office bought portable posts with retractable webbing belts; these were used to define a line where the queue would form. Now everyone who wanted service was held in the same line in the order of their arrival. As the person at the head of the queue was called forward for service, the line would move up. Not only was this process seen by customers to be fair and orderly, it also removed the dramatic variation in waiting times.

The difference now was that while I had all of the customers who wanted service in front of me, I also had all of the available serving staff

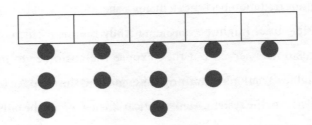

Traditional multiple queue

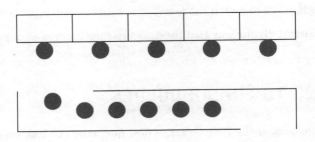

Single linear queue

serving us. The effect of this was to average the waiting time. Everyone would wait about the same length of time – typically less than twice the average transaction time – and no one customer would be subjected to a lengthy wait. (Supermarkets – are you following this?)

The customer reaction was overwhelmingly positive. This was much better. I spent time in stores watching how the process worked

22

and talked to staff and customers. One word was used more than any other to describe how customers felt about the situation: Fair. Customers don't mind waiting if the process of allocating service to them is seen to be fair.

We did the biggest branches first; as we rolled into smaller locations further issues became apparent. It was easy to buy a few barriers and put them in the middle of a huge space to create a line for people to stand in, but as soon as you started to work in smaller branches where space was at a premium, it became more difficult. In the old multiple-line situation it

> **CUSTOMERS DON'T MIND WAITING if the process of allocating service to them is seen to be fair.**

didn't matter – customers just stood where they could – space was the least of their worries when they were spending their time monitoring how much more quickly everyone else was getting served compared to them. But now suddenly it was important.

I quickly became an expert with a tape measure. The size of the queue system was a function of the number of people who would be waiting to be served, and how close together they would stand. I did some research around the UK and the results were surprising. Typically people waiting in a line in a post office would stand about 60 cm (around two feet) away from one another. But there was also some variation between cultures and different parts of the country – in southwest Scotland, for example, people stood nearly three feet or a metre apart.

The lines of barriers also needed to be a certain width apart, to allow pushchairs and wheelchairs unimpeded access. Using these broad calculations we could start to get some science into the number of barriers each branch needed and how best to lay them out. (We found that signs on the posts at the start and end of the queue helped customers understand what to do at the various points – all of which contributed to removing stress from the situation and getting people into the right mood to be served.)

This experience was useful for me later when purchasing departments of all flavours would ring me, "What's your best price on 500 barriers?" My response was invariably, "How do you know you need 500? Why not 600 or 200? If I can achieve what you need with only 300 I will save you 40% of your budget – shall we start there?"

THE DAWNING OF A DISCIPLINE?

The roots of a science were starting to emerge – not just an understanding of how to improve the lot of waiting customers, but an understanding of how much space was required and how to marshal available resources to get the best result. We had made it feel fairer and nicer; what else could we do?

Defining a difficulty

One problem emerged around the use of the linear queue in Post Office branches – one small dark cloud in an otherwise sunny skyline.

At that time all post offices used "fortress counters," where each cashier sat behind a service window. The glass made it difficult for waiting customers to hear or see when a cashier summoned them.

This led to occasional moments of comedy. Imagine. Customer stands at the head of the line, complacently staring into space. At the far end of the counter, the cashier is trying to attract his attention. But no matter how much the cashier yells or waves his arms about, the impenetrable glass transforms his best efforts into a silent ballet – the customer remains oblivious. This situation was normally relieved by another member of the queue noticing and tapping the daydreaming customer on the shoulder and pointing out the free counter.

Not only was this embarrassing for the customer and inhibiting for the staff, it slowed down the action. All the time that this was going on the line was not moving forward. Precious staff hours were being lost in idle time when they could have been used for serving.

How could we change this?

Solving the problem

In the early 90s digital technology created the promise of making and playing back high-quality sound recordings in a way which had not previously been possible. This novel technology converged with my work with the Post Office and an idea was born.

A display could be installed at the head of the queue with a voice that would prompt customers when a cashier was ready. It seemed to us that this would make the queue flow more smoothly and improve the experience for both staff and customers.

The Post Office had tried other ways to do this before, and there were also a number of display solutions on the market at the time – but none of them quite did the job.

An earlier system relied on sensors to call waiting customers to the counters: A sensor at each serving position monitored whether it was occupied or vacant, while a sensor at the head of the queue monitored if there were any customers waiting. When the system detected someone waiting, a display at the head of the queue would flash an instruction to move to one of the vacant serving positions. There

> BECAUSE PEOPLE rarely stand perfectly still, the sensors would erroneously detect a vacant position.

were several problems with this, however. On a cold day, people coming into the post office wearing dark clothes (which seemed to retain the cold longest) would not be picked up by the sensors monitoring the queue, and would therefore be "invisible" to the system; they could find themselves waiting at head of queue and, although positions were available, not be called forward because the sensor could not detect them. The sensors at the serving positions also had trouble detecting customers standing there. Because people rarely stand perfectly still, the sensors would erroneously detect a vacant position and the system would call another customer forward when one was still being served. To make matters worse, as the system was driven "automatically," it had no knowledge of impending staff breaks or end of shift, and so would relentlessly call customers forward. This was not a success.

Another system had the display at the head of the queue showing all of the positions that were currently free. Confronted with a choice, what does a customer do? He hesitates – again slowing the system down.

What was obvious from this analysis was that just because you put some electronics together in a box and called it a system it didn't necessarily make things better. It was important to understand the essence of what was failing before attempting to create a solution. Any other approach would lead to a flop. This needed to be based on first hand observation and not third-hand opinion. Facts not supposition. In our case it was essential to carry out detailed and rigorous

> **CONFRONTED WITH A CHOICE, what does a customer do? He hesitates – again slowing the system down.**

observation at each stage, looking at branches of different types and size, looking at existing "solutions" in the market place, and then defining the rules for the approach that we would take. This is how we created our customer-centric solution.

CASHIER NUMBER THREE PLEASE!

It was clear to us that linear queues needed a better system of summoning the next customer. The system should give one instruction at a time, and as far as possible should sound like the person who was about to serve you – hence the high-quality voice recordings and playback, and the use of male and female voices. (Usually men choose the male voice and women the female; however there was at least one office I visited where they liked to mix it up.) The system should make customers go "Wow," and make life easier for the hard-pressed staff in the branch.

Hence the idea for the Call Forward System – "Cashier Number Three Please!" – was born.

"Don't know why someone didn't come up with it before," people would say. Which I took to be a vast compliment. It meant that the system didn't feel alien, and it slotted right into our perceived gap where a solution needed to be.

We had captured people's hearts and minds with our idea but it still took two, very patient, years for our small team to move from observation to installing our first prototype system in a Post Office branch. And that nearly didn't happen.

GOING TO TRIAL

It was a spring morning in Central London. My walk from the train station to the Post Office headquarters was refreshing, and allowed me to focus on the objectives for the important meeting that lay ahead. Today was critical because it was decision time: Would the Post Office sign up to put our prototype into a branch?

We had reached a crucial moment in piloting our project from concept to reality. From early observation, we had analysed the current situation in the branch, and drafted a specification for our solution. This had been successfully debated with a series of groups of Post Office management and staff. It was important to us to have all of our stakeholders on board both at an executive and operational level so that this project could progress smoothly. As this process went on in the "front of house," in the back room our rocket scientists were designing

> **The system should make the customers go "WOW!"**

circuitry and solving the myriad of puzzles required to turn the idea into a real system.

Around the highly polished boardroom table sat fifteen people. My colleagues were on hand to demonstrate our technology to the gathering of senior management from the Post Office – among whom was the manager of a major city-centre branch. He had come to the meeting with the impression that his opinion was wanted about the solution; but as the meeting progressed it became apparent to him that something more would be expected of him. He was not happy.

After a series of presentations which brought everyone up to date with the project, and then a demonstration of the system – which was greeted with much enthusiasm – we reached the critical stage of the meeting. Our manager was put on the spot. He was asked to trial the system in his branch.

All eyes were on him. As the meeting had progressed our man had become more and more withdrawn. Now his legs were crossed and his arms folded. The question hung in the air.

With trembling lips he finally spoke. "My team work really hard to deliver great service and our customers are very happy with us. I don't believe that any system can improve upon that. I don't want it. It will never work."

There was a general sharp intake of breath followed by an expectant and embarrassed silence.

Was that it? After two years of hard work, was it all to end here in this meeting? There must be something I could say which would turn the thing around? What was it? My mind raced to develop the persuasive arguments that would convince our doubting manager to work with us.

Before I could speak, however, our Post Office project manager, who had been with us from the start of the project, piped up. Quietly and eloquently he explained that the whole point of the trial was to establish within a well-run office whether the new system could indeed improve customer service, and that we needed a manager who would be constructively critical of the system and not just accept it as the new status quo. The day was saved.

> **WAS THAT IT? After two years of hard work, was it all to end here in this meeting?**

NEVER BELIEVE AN "AHH-BUTTER"

Attitude is a funny thing. A psychologist once introduced me to the "Ahh-Butter" concept. No, not the stuff you spread on your toast, but someone who, when confronted with a new idea says "Ah – But…" – and usually followed by something along the lines of "we tried that five years ago and it didn't work then."

A single "Ahh-Butter" within a group of six is enough to stop any progress happening for years.

The psychologist explained to me that people, particularly people we call managers, are often frightened of change. Their whole career has brought them to a point where they feel that they have some control over their destiny, and this is based on their confidence in their own ability to supervise and manage the efforts of their team and the results that they produce. Change, however, is an external factor. If they don't introduce it, they don't control it. That's why it's scary, and people's reaction is to neutralise it.

But if managers can be made to feel that they are in control of that change, able to influence its direction or stop it completely, they will not fear that change. And once they get their confidence back, things can move on apace. By tackling people's fear of change you enable them to play an active role in its management.

That's what happened to our branch manager. He was persuaded by the reassurance of his authority within the process, by being listened to rather than talked at and ultimately by the evidence of his own eyes and ears as his customers and staff gave him feedback about the new system. He owned the solution and was proud of it.

THE VERY FIRST INSTALLATION

Our team worked the whole weekend to install that first prototype system in the manager's branch. Much later, when the system moved into production, installation of the systems would take less than six hours, but for this very first system – which was pretty much a proof of concept – serious engineering effort and not a little blood, sweat and tears were required to ensure that everything was working to perfection by the time the Post Office team arrived for work on Monday morning.

We were there at 7.30 a.m. to demonstrate the system to the staff and show them how to operate it. They took to it with ease and with delight. We waited in the branch office for the doors to open. It was one of those moments of truth that you face in your life. Everything was in place and there was nothing else that I could do to influence the outcome. I felt like the novice comedian wondering how the audience would react to his first gag. How would customers who had never seen this system react? Would they love it? Or would they hate it?

At 8.30 a.m., the manager opened the heavy oak doors. Customers streamed in. I stood in a corner with the project manager. We watched as my voice sounded from the display for the very first time anywhere. It was position number three that was called first, hence "Cashier Number Three Please" stuck as the name for the new system. All was sweetness and light. The staff took to the new system like it had always been there. Customers went through the queue impassively, waiting their turn and then moving promptly to each position as they were called. The whole thing worked like clockwork.

> **IT WAS POSITION THREE** that was called first, and "Cashier Number Three Please" stuck as the name for the new system.

I was desperate to get a waiting customer's opinion; what did they really think of it? As if on cue an elderly lady who had been through the line, been served and was now leaving the office approached the part of the office where I and my colleague from Post Office were standing. He was wearing a prominent badge on his lapel and so she came and stood directly in front of him.

"Young man! Do you work for the Post Office? This new system that you have installed? Best thing you have ever done. Well done!"

And off she strode into the sunset. Our heroine.

Within days the branch manager was receiving praise from staff and customers for the new system; a significant number of customers actually wrote to him thanking him for installing the system. He was converted. He became the best "sales persuader" we ever had. Whenever we talked to a new prospect we would send them to review the installation in that office and to meet "our" branch manager.

EXPLOITING AN IDEA SUCCESSFULLY

We had a success on our hands. Through our rigorous approach we had developed an idea which stood the test of use in the branch. Everyone was delighted. Over the years I have reflected many times not only on what we achieved but also how we achieved it. It seems to me that there were a number of necessary conditions that had to be met in order for this approach to be successful:

1. Understand the opportunity

The first stage was to define the problem by gaining a thorough understanding of what really happened in the branches through first-hand observation and interviews. Each facet of the argument needed to be supported by hard evidence – what made us so sure that we understood the situation and that we had an idea that would be successful?

2. Define the scope

We estimated from this process that we could not only improve the waiting customers' perception of their experience, but also make the queue move faster by reducing the idle moments when the cashiers were forced to wait for the next customer to arrive in front of them from the head of queue. We also assessed that the problem was universal, applying to many linear queue situations, ensuring a sizable market opportunity for our solution.

3. Define your investment and payback

You need to be able to estimate the cost of the resources required to fully develop your idea and take it to market as well as the unit cost and likely revenue potential. Revenue can generally be estimated by considering the cost of the problem that is being solved and creating a "return on investment" model for purchase. Be careful, it's easy to underestimate the cost of getting an idea to market. Generally it takes about seven times the cost of the original idea to put the first real one in the hands of a customer.

4. Sell the idea

Next it was necessary to convince our target client, Post Office, not only of the validity of the argument but also to trust us to work with them to create the solution. Commercially we did this by bearing the financial cost of developing the solution ourselves, limiting Post Office's cost to management time and intellectual effort. The in-branch trial was a vital milestone in this process and needed to be proactively managed to ensure a successful outcome.

5. Get a partner

When the Post Office decided they wanted to roll out such a system, they quite rightly ran a commercial tender process, inviting a range of organisations to submit their ideas and prices for a solution to the identified need. As part of our submission we offered to pay a commission to Post Office for every system we sold to another bank or retailer for the first five years, to recognise their "investment" of time, thought and reputation. In the process we recruited a sales ally – an organisation who would willingly endorse our offer to third parties and pass enquiries to us.

6. Cultivate your stakeholders

For this process to work there has to be a champion inside the customer's organisation who has the vision to perceive the future benefits of the proposal and who is prepared to sell it to his board and his colleagues. There has to be a clear understanding of who all of the stakeholders in the project are and what a win looks like for them individually, what's everyone's motivation for involving themselves ("What's in it for me?"). Each stakeholder needs to have a sense of ownership of the project which comes from involvement and the feeling that they have real influence over its direction. Regular communication is key to maintaining everyone's motivation as well as making real progress across the team. Agreed actions should

YOUR CUSTOMER WINS by getting a free "new ideas" department at almost no cost.

always be minuted so that the whole group are clear about who is making what contribution and whether they are on schedule. The good opinion of the group becomes the reason why people make progress when they could claim that they are busy on other things. Provided everyone remains positive and highly enthusiastic, no one will want to be seen to be holding things up. Communication, enthusiasm, attention to detail and follow up are watchwords of progress.

7. Challenge the value you are creating

For the supplier, this process helps you to clearly identify your customers' perceived need but also to challenge it with common sense. Is it a real need or just someone's hobbyhorse? You need to keep asking the same question. How will this benefit the business (the staff, the customers etc.)? Maintain the team's focus on the benefits of the solution and not on the features. It doesn't matter how clever the technology, unless it leads through to a tangible benefit it will remain unsaleable. Keeping communication global, across all stakeholders in the customers' organisation will ensure that the project is not hijacked by one stakeholder whose views would misrepresent the customers' true needs.

If you follow this process as partners, both organisations derive tangible benefits.

Your customer wins by getting a free "new ideas" department at almost no cost – and with strictly limited risk. It amazes me how few organisations take this opportunity up.

As a supplier you will have a clearly differentiated solution to offer to your customer and a partner who sees you as a vital part of their team.

For us, Qm and the Post Office, the quality that underpinned this process most was mutual trust. Both organisations found a way to work together for their mutual benefit, creating a solution that had never existed before and overcoming all obstacles along the way.

I owe my business success to the Post Office. Without their backing for "Cashier Number Three Please," Qm would never have existed; we wouldn't have created 75 jobs in the UK; and I would not have gone on to be a board member of a global company, Qmatic Group.

The Post Office may not be foremost in the general public's mind when the discussion turns to innovation but my experience of the organisation as a customer and business partner has shown that there are few brands in the UK who can match them for their willingness to listen to new ideas and their application in applying them.

Innovation, by which I mean the successful exploitation of ideas, involves change and risk. Managers are needed to manage risk down to acceptable levels. I call the process we followed Task-centric Innovation: focussing a tightly managed group of stakeholders, each with relevant knowledge and experience, onto a precisely defined problem or opportunity. Once you have managed the risk down as far as you can, what's left is blind faith, the power to persuade yourself, your team and your customer to back your judgement.

This was the first time we did it but by no means the last.

04

BANKING
ON A QUEUE

STORMING THE BANKS

"Cashier Number Three Please!" really did seem to add something to the way the Post Office branches worked. When we phoned an office to tell them that funds were now available to install their Call Forward System, they would get very excited and grateful.

It was time to seek more customers. Could we persuade others that they too would benefit from our solution? Where, other than the post office, did people have to wait in lines and had lots of branches?

The banks.

We wrote to them. We telephoned them. We pursued them. And finally we got an appointment – with the Chief Architect at a Major Bank, headquartered in a lofty tower in London.

We arrived for our appointment. There were three of us, and just as well because we had to carry our demo rig, which was too big for the lift, up four flights of stairs to reach the gentleman's office.

I tend to talk with my hands, and when I am presenting, whole arms go flying around. Well with everything set up and now with four of us in this office it was cosy to say the least. I had to keep one hand in my pocket as I presented. Both barrels for 20 minutes. At the end of which the gentleman took off his glasses and studied his fountain pen.

"Yes," he said (to the fountain pen). "What a good idea, very interesting." Pause. "And if we had problems with queues I would most definitely be interested!"

Much later, on our way home, I had a chance to cool down and reflect on this outcome. Although I had pitched a solution that I believed was needed in the bank's branches, the reality was that the banks at that time just didn't get it. Queueing was not on their radar. They saw it as a given. If you had branches, you had queues. Period.

In my enthusiasm I had lost sight of the fact that organisations rarely buy "nice-to-haves." You have to find the thing that's hurting – where is the stone in the shoe? If you can sell against that need you are on to a winner.

I decided to go back to watching customers and staff in the post office and contrasting what was happening in the branches that now had Call Forward with those that had not yet acquired it. Could I draw out evidence that would help me per- **Organisations rarely buy "NICE-TO-HAVES."** suade the banks that they needed us? I needed to re-ask the questions: What had we achieved? Why were post offices so positive towards the system? How could I turn this positivity into a sales pitch?

So off I went to lurk in branches once more and mine for nuggets of presentational gold.

I HEAR VOICES

When the Post Office moved from multiple lines to a single queue they made the process of getting access to service in the branches feel fair. This

41

was a revelation. At a fundamental level they changed the way shoppers felt about waiting. The change in methodology also removed the wild swings in waiting time that customers experienced in their branches, making it feel even better. Complaints went down, stress levels dropped and customers were much happier to wait.

Adding the Call Forward System improved things further. It took a lot of "waste" out of the service system. By alerting customers as quickly and effectively as possible when a cashier became free to serve them, it kept things moving along at a rapid pace. Staff controlled the process. There were no sensors to deliver spurious calls; the servers simply pushed a button when they were ready to see someone. The system provided the means to get a message to the customer where they were waiting, through an audio-visual display directly in front of them. Customers and staff reaction to this system was highly positive, but the reasons for this only became obvious on close examination.

When someone talks to you it is the most natural thing in the world to look towards the source of the voice. A natural-sounding voice delivered from a visual display meant that waiting customers would assimilate the message fast.

By watching the way customers and staff behaved and continuously refining the system, we were able to speed up the queue. We could deliver a polite message that sounded relaxed in a four-second cycle: voice, flashing main display, flashing positional display. When necessary we could cut down this cycle to one-and-a-half seconds to get people through the queue faster.

The use of the voice had some powerful effects that we hadn't anticipated. Subconsciously, customers in the store would get a sense of the pace of service by hearing the voice sound off every time a customer was called forward – even though we tuned the volume to be audible to the customers at the head of the line but unobtrusive to others in the store, including the staff, who would otherwise have to listen to it all day. We found that the voice set the rhythm of the queue. Similar to the effect of playing upbeat music in fast-food restaurants, waiting customers responded to the pace by walking more quickly when the store was busy and they heard the voice sound more often. Another unexpected effect was that as the queue moved faster it became "stickier," i.e., if people got the sense that the queue would move rapidly, they were more likely to join the queue, and less likely to desert it once they were there.

Installing the system in other locations reinforced the results. In Irish post offices, customers thought the branch provided a better and more pleasant experience. When, much later, we installed the system with the US Postal Service Branch at the James Farley Building in New York, my rough timing of the line before and after installation suggested customers got served 36% faster, while with a major bank in Dublin we saw a 63% reduction in waiting times.

It was only after quite a few years of watching such situations that I was asked by one retailer to compare our solution directly with that of a competitor. I learned something from this situation that just hadn't dawned on me before. Although it might sound like heresy coming from me, putting in a queueing system doesn't always make things better. Not all Call Forward systems were born equal. Ours worked, by which I mean that the staff kept using it, and the staff and customers appreciated the difference it made. Our formula of high-quality voice, delivered from a display that provided a simple, fast visual message, was absorbed intuitively by waiting customers and they moved promptly to the right desk for service.

The main errors that our competitors made fell into two camps, which I christened "The Voice of God" and "The Voice in a Cupboard." The Voice of God is where the supplier mounts the speakers in the ceiling somewhere above the head of the queue. As soon as the voice sounds, the waiting customers look straight up – away from the display and the counter. By the time they look back, the numbers have stopped flashing and the server has to push the button again. This can happen several times before anyone gets served. It's not very efficient. The Voice in a Cupboard is where a supplier uses an unsuitable voice, recorded in a sub-standard way, and delivered through a poor speaker. The effect is like a really bad railway announcement. You know that someone is saying something, but who knows what? In both cases these attempts actually slow the queue down, because the customer at the front of the queue hesitates while trying to work out what's going on and where they are supposed to be. The staff stop relying on the system because it makes their job harder and slows things down. Pretty soon they are back to shouting, "Next customer!" and the system gathers dust and undermines the reputation of all queue management.

> THE MAIN ERRORS our competitors made: The Voice of God, and The Voice in the Cupboard.

This reinvigorated my sales efforts. It was clear to me that what we did made things better – for staff and for consumers alike. Armed with the courage of my convictions, I renewed my efforts to persuade the banks to join us.

GOING ON THE OFFENSIVE

We started offering a "Try Before You Buy" demonstration facility. This allowed new customers to have a system installed, for up to 90 days, so that their staff and customers could sample its delights before they paid for it. Known in the sales trade as a Puppy Dog Sale (once you get the puppy in your arms you don't want to give it back), we found this to be a great "risk-free" way for organisations to feel the benefits for themselves.

We made slow but steady progress, and all the time more and more of the top tier of the Post Office network – the busy Crown Offices – were going linear and receiving their Call Forward System.

To really target the banks, we developed a multi-level mailing technique. Level One was the branch managers of big, old bank branches in city centres – the ones most likely to have queueing issues and, importantly, near to post offices with "Cashier Number Three Please" recently installed. At the same time we would write to Levels Two and Three – the branch's area management, and the purchasing office. The intention was quite simple. I wanted to initiate a dialogue between the interested parties. Imagine the scenario. Branch manager receives mailing and raises it with his area manager: "This is just the thing we need in our office. We have that awkward pillar that people waiting in line can't see around when a teller comes free." Area manager endorses the view – "I've seen something about this" – and passes it through to purchasing, who now have three sets of our sales literature, and take it seriously on the word of their own people. We started to make real progress.

As the banks realised that we made lives easier in their larger, older legacy branches, they came to embrace our system. Queueing-related complaints plummeted.

There was another unseen factor that had a huge multiplier effect on our sales efforts: the Great British Public – our unsung heroes. Something like 80% of the Post Office's customers used their branch once a week, and they loved "Cashier Number Three Please." It made their lives easier and speeded up the wait. They did us a great favour. They went from the post office into their bank and said to the staff, "Why don't you have a system like the one in the post office? It's so much better than in here."

So while the market for our solution was initiated and driven by us, market adoption was turbo-charged by our customers' customers, the real beneficiaries of what we had created. They loved it and they helped make our business what it is today.

I actually had one bank's purchasing office ring me and say, "We hate you."

"Sorry?" I said.

"We hate you because we now have to buy these systems from you and there is no way back. Our customers are demanding that we make the queues in our branches work better."

Consumer power really works.

The early adopters in the banking sector were rewarded by happier customers who returned to the branch more often and complained less. The laggards were punished by their customers, assaulted with phone calls and letters berating them to invest in the service. It took a while but sooner or later everyone caught on.

I knew that we had made it into popular culture when one night on his BBC talk show Jonathan Ross was interviewing Roger Moore. "So Roger, you have fallen on hard times then?" (Roger looks affluent and puzzled.) "That is your voice in the post office doing "Cashier Number Three," isn't it?"

We have tried to spread the fame around. There are now quite a number of much more talented voice artists who have added to the "Cashier Number Three Please!" library.

A couple of years ago, inspired by the popularity of various TV series, we held a "Queue Idol" competition in Ireland. It ran as a phone-in in which over 3,000 callers cast their votes, and four voices were eventually selected to be heard several million times a month across Northern Ireland and Ireland.

The UK Post Office has continued to be an innovator in queue management. In recent years as part of a business strategy to update their branches and move away from their legacy locations, they have introduced virtual queueing to around 60 new concept locations. Working closely with Qmatic and their design agency, they installed a new "check-in process," allowing customers to reserve their turn for counter services. In these locations it is no longer necessary for customers to wait in line; they are free to browse the store, and to make other purchases, while they wait in a virtual queue. The Post Office is furthermore able to use the data that the system collects, to better understand how customers want to use their branch, and hence improve service delivery.

05

STANDING IN LINE
VS. TAKING A
TICKET

VIRTUAL QUEUEING

While we were having all this fun in the UK with linear queues, our opposite numbers in Sweden were developing their business model around what we now call "virtual queueing." With linear queues, customers join the back of a line and are called for service on a "first in, first out" basis. With virtual queues there is no need to stand in any particular place, as your turn for service is reserved by some other means. It could be that customers take a numbered ticket on arrival, or maybe they leave their name with a receptionist, or they are given a pager to walk around with which will buzz to bring them back to the service point.

In Sweden, some ten years before we were making "Cashier Number Three Please" a reality of the UK High Street, Qmatic was founded by an engineer and a service-minded entrepreneur running a restaurant business in Gothenburg. The entrepreneur, Rune Sahlin, invented a number-and-display system enabling customers to choose their meal and see when it was their turn to collect it. This was the first Qmatic system. The company soon started installing systems in the Swedish Post Office, banks and major railway stations. As we in Britain were getting used to the sound of "Cashier Number Three Please," in Scandinavia it became second nature to take a ticket to reserve your turn for service. Further product development propelled Qmatic into supplying its solutions across the world.

To this day, most retail environments and banking halls in Scandinavia feature some form of virtual queueing system, as do many countries across Europe. Equally, in other parts of the world the linear queue is the accepted standard for organising the waiting process.

Is one better than the other? There are still some who believe that one methodology, either linear queue or virtual queue, is superior. I have heard many heated debates about this. In reality both are valid and have their place. It is a question of context. The right methodology will speed things up and make the whole thing feel nicer for staff and waiting consumers. The wrong one slows things down and, worse still, upsets people.

> NO BLOOD BANKS make their customers wait in line – all use a ticket system.

It is true that linear queueing is more obviously present in Anglo-Saxon cultures while virtual queueing has spread more generally across continental Europe and many non-English-speaking countries. But this is way too simplistic an analysis. Pretty much every airport around the world uses linear queues to manage check-in and security screening. In the same way, I haven't seen a hospital blood bank anywhere in the world that makes their customers wait in line – all use a ticket system. The reality is that both methodologies are in use in almost all nations of the world.

ACCEPTED BEHAVIOUR

There are cultural differences between nations that need to be understood and respected; these affect the decision as to how to organise necessary waits for service. At the simplest level watch the way people organise themselves as they wait for a bus. Do they stand in a kind of self-selecting line and get on the bus in a "first in, first out" manner or do they go forward together in a mass huddle with a much less obvious precedence? These things are important in determining how best to implement solutions that both customers and staff will view positively. The closer that a system mimics the way people are used to behaving the more likely it is to be successfully adopted.

There are many parts of the world where the accepted practice for waiting doesn't involve standing in line, and it's seen as perfectly acceptable to crowd and jostle to reach the front sooner than those who arrived earlier. This Darwinesque approach to waiting – the fittest get served first – exists in all countries, including the UK, when circumstances dictate.

I read a newspaper article a couple of years ago which took an interesting line on linear queueing. It delved back into our ancestry of warring tribes to suggest that under the British veneer of civilized waiting behaviour there lurks a dark psyche. In essence, we are all at heart axe-wielding warriors, and if anyone attempts to jump the queue, blood will be shed. Professor Richard Larson at MIT talks about "slips and skips" in the waiting process, where, if

UNDER THE BRITISH VENEER of civilised waiting behaviour lurks a dark psyche.

it's possible for an individual to cheat the waiting system and "skip" into a position ahead of their rightful place in the queue, then the resultant "slip" for the rest of us who are waiting patiently results in a dis-benefit which is felt pretty hard by all concerned.[2]

You can see the evidence of this with your own eyes. Join any linear queue and watch what happens when someone tries to push in. It takes a very thick-skinned individual to be able to successfully accomplish this task and endure the silent fury of other waiting individuals who feel that they have lost out.

Will this turn us cool-blooded, stiff-upper-lipped Brits into homicidal maniacs? Probably not – though in recent years a number of instances of "queue rage" have made the national press. In these reports some act of violence followed someone pushing in ahead of their turn. Although the exception, such incidents are indicative of the fact that consumers in general are becoming less tolerant of situations that they see as being patently inequitable and where they experience bad service.

In the late 90s we worked with Argos, the UK catalogue retailer, to install a "Take a ticket" system to manage the wait at their jewellery counter. This simple solution was rapidly installed in pretty much all of their stores. A few months after the roll-out was complete, I asked the Argos team for their views of the solution in preparation for the writing of a press release. "How has it benefited your business?" I naively asked. The answer I expected was something along the lines of, "Well, customers like it because it allows them to reserve their turn for service and keep browsing" or some such thing. In fact the response was a little more edgy: "At Christmas, when the stores are busy, our staff can now serve customers rather than break up fights."

> AT CHRISTMAS, when the stores are busy, our staff can now serve customers rather than break up fights.

A MATTER OF CONTEXT

Managing payment at the end of shoppers' transactions is probably the biggest area that we have influenced so far in retail, particularly in the UK and USA. A linear queue system has become the accepted standard for cash-taking in most stores. "Cashier Number Three Please!" has been widely adopted in the UK because it really does tune up the service process and help to get people through as quickly as possible while making it "feel nicer" for the waiting customers.

Linear queues work best when each customer's transaction is relatively short, say, less than seven minutes. The shorter the average transaction time, the more appropriate a linear queue is. As we saw at the Post Office, a linear queue triumphs when there is a big variation in how long it takes to serve each customer; with multiple lines I am the hapless victim of the customers waiting in front of me, whose tasks are unknowable and must all be served before me. The chances are that the lines around me will move faster than mine.

> **LINEAR QUEUES work best when each customer's transaction is relatively short.**

So a single line of waiting customers, with all staff serving one queue will make a longer line that moves much faster. The line of customers waits close to the counter where they will be served and so the walk time from the queue to the counter is kept to a minimum, keeping the efficiency of the process high.

In general, virtual queues suit situations where either the transactions take longer (and therefore the waiting time will almost certainly be longer) or it's a good idea to keep people mobile, to move around, or take a seat. Using a virtual queue system can also make sense when there is a need to serve people in an order other than "first in, first out" – as we shall see in later chapters. It also lends itself to capturing time-stamped data about customer arrivals, making it easy to measure waiting times.

The disadvantage of virtual queues is that it generally takes longer to get people back to the counter to serve them once they are called. This has implications for server efficiency – that's why it's better to use virtual queues for longer transactions, where the longer delay between calling a customer and their arrival at the service position is less of an issue.

06

THE
IMPULSE
BUY

ENHANCING THE QUEUEING EXPERIENCE

In 2000, with linear queues now being widely used for cash-taking, we went a stage further. Although our solutions were popular with shoppers, persuading retailers to part with the money to improve things was more difficult. We had gradually developed our "value proposition" based on (a) enriched customer experience, leading to greater customer loyalty, and (b) increased efficiency, i.e. being able to serve more customers for a given number of staff hours. But how could we really convince the retailers? Could we make the queueing system pay for itself? Was there a way to keep customers shopping while they were waiting to pay?

The idea of In-Queue Impulse Merchandising was born.

There was nothing new about putting merchandise at the registers; supermarkets and other retailers had been doing it for a long time. But no one had put it back along the line where people were standing.

The more I thought about this the more sense it made. By the time people got to the register, it was too late to present products to them. At the counter they were focussed on handing over their goods, paying and leaving. All that merchandise around the till just created clutter. I wonder how many retailers have stood back and taken a good look at their payment area. Racks of gum and confectionery at eye height and knee height (why does anyone think that would work?) facing the customer, so that the cashiers have to peer out from a forest of stuff. That's just not right.

It seemed to me that if we instead put the merchandise back into the line – where people were waiting – there was just a chance we could increase sales of small impulse items, without adding to the clutter.

GETTING IT RIGHT

Queues are typically organised so that customers stand in a line parallel with the row of cash registers. Because most shoppers are right-handed, the ideal situation is to have the head of the line at the left-hand end of the registers; this allows the next customer who will be served to line up opposite Register 1, and then read the register numbers from left to right. This is the easiest and therefore fastest way for customers to assimilate where the free service position is.

As queues aren't full all of the time, those retailers who put merchandise all the way along both sides of the queue barrier are building slow-moving stock. The best sales area is the last two metres of queue barrier situated between the line of waiting customers and the registers.

This area of the queue barrier is the most compelling shopping zone because of a couple of factors. The first is that it is the busiest part of the queue line, and generally has several people standing next to it -- so maximum proximity to waiting shoppers. Second, waiting customers tend to subconsciously glance across at the registers where they will be served, and so presenting the merchandise between them and the registers puts it in their field of vision. (I have found only one exception to this, and that's when customers are waiting to pay in a fuel station; instead of looking at

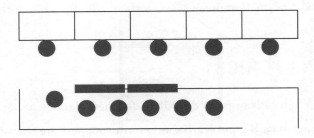

Positioning impulse merchandising in the linear queue

the registers most look out of the windows at their cars – which is why all of those tempting chocolate bars are racked up under the windows!)

Now that we had decided where to put the merchandise the next question was how best to display it? Over the years I have seen this done so badly it's a wonder anything ever gets sold. Typically stores will use flat shelving between the barriers, and there will be up to five levels between the floor and waist height, which the retailer will pack with merchandise. Have these people never stood in their own queue? People in queues don't stand facing the shelves; they stand alongside them, and close to them. When they look across the shelving all they see is the top shelf or two – everything else is invisible. Do retail designers think that their shoppers will get so carried away that they will put down their basket and start hunting around the bottom shelves? Paco Underhill documented

60

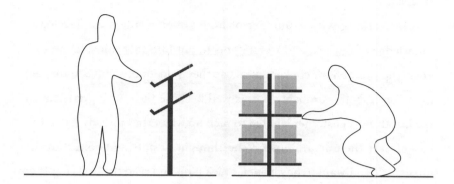

Designing impulse merchandising

this phenomenon and coined a phrase for it: the "Butt Brush" -- shoppers are disinclined to bend over where it's likely that there will be someone immediately behind them.

To properly design impulse merchandising, consider the average height of the shopper. Now, without the shopper bending at the waist, consider the natural span of their arms and their field of vision when they look alongside them and down. That's the right zone for impulse merchandising in queues.

THE PAYBACK

Argos was the first retailer to do this with us and the system we put in place was a phenomenal success. It paid for itself in just nine weeks. It was so good that extra staff hours had to be created to keep the queue system stocked.

In working with a number of high-street retailers we developed knowledge of the best and worst items to put into this valuable impulse area. The worst? Slow cookers. Because they were bulky, you couldn't get many on a shelf – probably just as well because they were pretty much the last thing a customer wanted to pick up when they already had a full basket over their arm. Books. Who thought of putting books into the queue? When I want to buy a book I pick it up and read the first couple of pages. Probably I will then put it back and do the same with another and another until I find one that's compelling. This process takes minutes, during which time I am pretty much dead to the world. Sounds like a great way to hold up the queue.

Items for impulse merchandising need to be of the point-and-grunt variety. Chewing gum, batteries, confectionery, bottled water, small packets of tissues – things that you would have bought as you went around the store had you noticed and wanted them. With this knowledge, we had some amazing results: a 700% increase in bottled water sales in a railway station newsagents, and 400% increase in battery sales.

ITEMS FOR IMPULSE merchandising need to be of the point-and-grunt variety.

Unfortunately, few retailers take the opportunity to serve us shoppers at this point in our journey through their store as seriously as they should. The worst offenders treat the queue as a dumping ground for marked-down merchandise that they could not sell elsewhere in the store. Insufficient thought is given to considering what items customers would like to see at this point. The smart retailers know how to dress the impulse-buy area with suitable promotional content, or seasonal fare, making it a pleasure for the waiting customer to keep shopping.

Developing our thinking around impulse merchandising allowed us to enhance our value proposition around the organisation of cash-taking. By optimising the linear queue we now realised that it was possible to enhance customer experience while saving valuable space and staff time as well as enhancing sales. This led to a major upswing in our linear queue for cash-taking business and made a major contribution to the company in the years leading up to our management buyout.

07

THE SCIENCE OF
QUEUENOMICS

EVERY TIME A CASHIER PRESSES the Call Forward button, a few things happen. A recorded voice announces, "Cashier Number Three Please"; the electronic signboard flashes the same message; and the lucky customer makes his way swiftly to the newly free window.

What also happens – behind the scenes – is that the time of each button-press is logged in the system. This means that Cashier Number Three's log retains a record of the times at which all his customers were served. More pertinently, we can see from the time-stamp intervals how long each customer's total service time was – how long they took to walk to the counter, plus how long they were served, plus any wasted "faffing time" at the transaction's end.

Such data was very useful to us when we were trying to understand the workings of queues.

One office's data delivered a useful insight. When we looked at their time-stamp data, something odd seemed to be happening. The data showed that customers who were served at the right-hand end of the counter always took longer than those served at the left. This made absolutely no sense to us. We checked our calculations. There it was again.

We met with the manager; did this make any sense to him? There was no obvious reason that he could think of. Still, the effect was there.

We stationed a volunteer behind the counter for a week to watch and see if we could work it out. It took a while but a pattern emerged. About every fourth transaction the cashiers needed a form to complete the work for that customer. All such paperwork was held in a carousel and the cashiers would have to get up from their serving position and walk to the carousel, get the form and bring it back to their position and complete it with the customer. The carousel was stationed at the left-hand end of the counter where the transactions appeared shortest.

NO ONE had noticed this. They were all busy just trying to serve customers as quickly as possible.

By installing a second carousel at the other end of the counter, we were able to equalise the transaction times across the cashiers and speed up the overall process of getting served in the post office.

No one had noticed this. They were all busy just trying to serve customers as quickly as possible. A classic case of "not seeing the wood for the trees."

CAPTURING DATA

My quest for knowledge started in the mid-90s, once we had an established base of post offices and a small but increasing number of bank branches. As our business grew there were questions that bugged me. Why did queues form? Were they in any way predictable, and if that was so, could we not eliminate them? How did queues affect customers' and staff attitudes and behaviours? Were there any rules that would help our clients to make it better and easier for the customers waiting in their stores?

While most organisations have good data (in theory) available within their cash register system about the serving process – how many operators, how many transactions, how long it takes to carry out certain functions – in practice the sheer size of the data-mining operation necessary to turn data into insight can make the task immeasurably difficult. The advantage of Call Forward, or indeed any queue management system, is the ability to provide this data through an independent stream, revealing just enough insight to persuade people to dig deeper into their systems.

The Post Office supported our attempts to gain a better understanding of the metrics around the queueing process. What helped us enormously was their mystery shopping operations – one of the most sophisticated being used anywhere in the UK – supported by a statistics department who really knew their stuff. Offices were sampled at different times of day according to a precise regime, which allowed Post Office HQ to understand typical demand levels across their estate of larger, directly managed Crown Offices. The data created by the mystery shopping operations allowed us to cross-check our own Call Forward data and prove its accuracy.

Our data became bankable, by being shown to be significantly better than the guesses that most organisations typically made to ascertain how long it took staff to achieve things. These guesses were often rooted in organisational folklore, and "tested" by means of stopwatch timings – where a consultant stood behind the member of staff and timed his or her work processes. (Being watched so closely, the staff members – consciously or subconsciously – either sped up in order to look like heroes or slowed down in order to give themselves more time.)

With these systems in place, we could capture and understand both the qualitative and quantitative aspects of face-to-face service delivery within the post offices. This helped us deliver efficiency gains and spot ways to make things better.

LEAN SERVICE DELIVERY?

There is a big difference between developing a lean manufacturing process and a lean process for the delivery of face-to-face service. In manufacturing, the supervisor generally has a schedule of what he plans to produce. A formal forecasting process drives the business, ensuring that everyone is working to the same plan. While some variation is tolerated, it is time critical: the closer the future point comes to today's production schedule, the firmer it has to be.

Delivering service to the public is a different game. It is possible to schedule an amount of future demand through appointment-setting – e.g. Apple's Genius Bars, the British Passport Office – but a large part of retailing in an affluent society is dealing with instantaneous demand. People want to shop when they want to shop and they don't necessarily want to plan it too far ahead. Balancing the supply of service with demand from shoppers in real time is an essential component of modern economies.

CALCULATING THE COST OF QUEUEING

It's a question of the economics of queues – Queuenomics. Can we estimate the total cost to the UK economy of providing service to shoppers –

and in fact all consumers who have to wait for anything, anywhere and anytime? And how efficiently is it delivered? Can we recognise the "opportunity costs" for both the organisations delivering service and the customers who have to wait for it?

Let's try it this way. Let's make an educated guess that the biggest food and non-food retailers – let's include the main banks here – have between them 20,000 locations in the UK where they deliver face-to-face service to their customers. On average the number of staff delivering face-to-face service in each branch is, say, ten. Now let's assume that the average total cost of each hour of each employee's time is £7.

£2.91 billion is invested by UK retailers and banks each year in providing face-to-face service to shoppers.

So that's 200,000 staff costing £7 per hour, or a total annual cost (at 40 hours a week for 52 weeks) of £2.91 billion. This is the estimated total amount invested by UK retailers and banks each year in delivering face-to-face service to shoppers.

Let's say that two-thirds of the UK population are active shoppers, shopping twice a week – that's 40 million people making 80 million unique shopping trips each week. That gives us 4 billion unique shopping trips per annum.

If on average we all have to wait five minutes to get served, that would mean 20 billion minutes, or a collective 5,000 years of people's time (in working weeks) spent waiting to be served every year.

Now if we could improve the efficiency of service allocation in stores by just 20% (perfectly doable – I have seen lots of situations where this has happened) then the suppliers of the service would achieve a combined saving of about £600 million, and consumers would get back 1,000 years of their collective working lives. Not once but every single year.

And that's just the private sector. The figures associated with the public sector are even larger. In total the UK's retail sector employs around 3 million people, while the UK's public sector employs about 8.3 million, including the National Health Service's 1.5 million.

In my calculation I estimated that 200,000 staff in retail were involved in delivering face-to-face service – about 6.66% of the total staff. In a bold and sweeping estimation let's assume that the proportions are similar in the public sector – 6.66% of 8.3 million is about 550,000. On the same cost per hour of £7, that's a public-sector face-to-face service commitment of £8 billion per annum. A 20% saving would put £1.6 billion worth of public sector hours back into the pot to be used more constructively for everyone's benefit.

Similarly there must be gains to be made in liberating unnecessary waiting times but these are harder to calculate as there is a much greater use of appointment-based systems in the public sector which would reduce the overall figures. That said, if we doubled our estimate of 1,000 people-years of unnecessary wait time, to 2,000 people-years for the whole economy, that seems like a conservative estimate.

That's 2,000 people-years of UK consumers' lives lost every year, and £2 billion of staff hours wasted, through bad queue management – surely our service-delivery organisations in the public and private sectors can do better than this?

PROACTIVE QUEUE MANAGEMENT

There are real and substantial benefits for us all to be gained by delivering better, faster service more efficiently across our economies.

- Public-sector organisations gain through more efficient service delivery and fewer reasons for complaints;
- Private-sector organisations gain competitive advantage in terms of increased operational efficiency and happier customers;
- Retail stores benefit through lowered costs, increased customer loyalty and basket size, and also do all of us a big favour in returning that most precious of our resources – time.

This is not an easy challenge but with the application of sound principles of queue management, major gains are possible.

Such efforts have to start with a profound understanding of the processes required to serve customers on a face-to-face basis and an acceptance that demand is customer-driven and not dictated by process capability. Organisations need to create service engines capable of responding proactively to real-time changes in demand. This is not about building high-cost service models but leaner organisations with open structures and staff who are trained, empowered and motivated to react to customer needs, working within environments which are designed to cope with likely customer demand levels.

> IT'S NOT JUST our wallets and our watches that are affected by waiting time.

It's not just our wallets and our watches that are affected by waiting time. Customers are deeply influenced by the way brands manage their waiting experience. If you create high-stress environments where I am left standing around for minutes on end and other customers could push in ahead of me then guess what? I don't enjoy it. What's more I am less likely to come back and do it again. I will punish you. I will buy less on this trip and I may tell all my friends how bad an experience I had.

The deeper I got into this subject the more I realised that the impact of waiting time was magnified by the circumstances that shoppers found themselves in. In fact, I often found that unless these were taken into account, data alone could seem to defy common sense.

For instance, take this office where we'd installed the Call Forward System. It's a busy period, and four staff are currently serving the customers. Each transaction is taking about four minutes on average, so the rate of flow through the queue is four minutes divided by four servers – one customer leaving the head of queue every minute. Now add another person serving. You would expect to see the flow rate of the queue increase by a factor of about 5/4, i.e., an increase of about 25% – but no, in fact the queue slows down. Why is this? Again we had to visit the branch and look at what really was happening to understand this unexpected outcome.

The staff came to work wanting to do the best job that they could. Sitting where they were at the counter, they could see the queue building up, so they served the customer in front of them as fast as they could. Some of the things that they would normally have done at the end of each transaction they held over for when it got quieter.

So when an extra member of the team joined them at the counter, it was like the cavalry coming over the hill – everyone breathed a sigh of relief. And slowed their pace. They caught up on the housekeeping that they should have done after each customer they had served. The flow rate of the queue dropped.

In time, if the branch became busy again, the service rate would recover – but the immediate impact on the queue length is negative.

The customers' reaction to this was just as unexpected. Although the pace of the queue had slowed, the fact that another member of staff had joined his colleagues to serve them showed that the staff were trying to get them served faster. Although the queue actually became longer nobody complained; they were focussed on the additional effort the staff were making and not on the speed of the queue.

> **WHEN AN EXTRA MEMBER joined them at the counter, it was like the cavalry coming over the hill.**

This was a staggering observation. It meant that the pure maths of queue management was only part of the equation. From a customer satisfaction point of view, managing the way that customers perceived what was going on was more important than serving them faster.

We now had extra dimensions to measure and think about in terms of store performance. Alongside the hard, measurable factors of transaction length, walking time, faffing time and number of staff serving, we now had "soft factors" as well: What impression were waiting customers getting from the efforts that staff made to serve them and how would this affect their behaviour in store now and in future?

08

BENDING
TIME

HAVING REALISED THE IMPORTANCE of "soft factors," I switched my research efforts from statistical data to behavioural models. I wanted to see if any scientific principles of queue management existed and how they would map onto my observations. If we could understand the mechanisms by which the systems that we installed worked we would be in a much better position to articulate the arguments for using them. We might also be able to quantify the benefits of what we had created and help our clients create "return-on-investment" arguments for their purchases.

Our competitors didn't seem to be troubled by any of these thoughts; they simply got on with the task of trying to sell the hardware of queue management. But it seemed to me fundamental.

I bought every book I could find with the word "queue" in the title. The works of David Maister and Professor Richard Larson chimed with my own experience and provided a backdrop when I was setting these thoughts out for the first time. David Maister's excellent analysis examined how the organisation of waiting time has a psychological effect on customers and their perceptions.[3] Richard Larson's paper delivered a comprehensive view of the available theory and helped me to appreciate the theoretical work that had gone into trying to understand queues.[4]

WHAT IT FEELS LIKE FOR A SHOPPER

I put my ideas into a "Blue Touch Paper" in 1997, so called because I wanted it to "ignite" people's thinking around the subject. Within a few weeks we had emailed, or sent by post, thousands of copies. They went far and wide to retailers, banks and airports all over the globe. It resonated with client and customer experience and helped to consolidate our thinking.

The paper was based on years of in-store observation and interviews with both staff and customers. I set out to get to the essence of the "soft factors" in queue management, the issues that make waiting acceptable to shoppers. Could I make tangible the way that it felt to be a shopper in a serving environment? Was it possible to articulate the factors which would help service-providers offer waiting customers a richer experience, so that they felt that it was a good – or at least acceptable – use of their time?

Five principles flowed from the analysis:

1. Customers will tolerate finite waiting times, provided those waiting times conform to the customers' notions of reasonableness.
2. Service allocation must always be seen to be fair.
3. Time spent waiting feels elastic; the degree of flex depends on how much frustration or delight the customer feels.
4. In managing wait times, the provider is dealing with the customer's perception, which may be very different from reality.
5. Queues represent a moment of truth; if managed well, they demonstrate a tangible commitment to customer service; if unplanned or unmanaged, they show contempt for the customer's time.

TOLERATING WAIT TIMES

Empirical research shows that customer are prepared to wait longer the more they value the service that they expect to receive. (This does not refer to the monetary value of the transaction, where, arguably, the consumer spending more will expect to be treated as more important and hence wait less.) This observation gives rise to the concept of relative time value. A waiting consumer will subconsciously allocate a value to his time and to that of the server, and adjust the period of tolerable waiting time accordingly.

Imagine two shoppers in very different circumstances. Our first shopper has a persistent cough that is keeping him awake at night, and decides to stop by a pharmacist's to get advice and medicine. The pharmacist is busy so the customer has to wait. The advice and medicine are important to him and this is the only pharmacist in town. He will therefore tolerate a significant wait in order to fix his cough. In fact, our sick shopper may even question the value of the advice that the pharmacist is about to give if there is no queue for his services.

> THE SOFT FACTORS of queue management: Issues that make waiting acceptable to shoppers.

Our second shopper is in the market for a new car. He has the money and is choosing between two prestigious models from competing manufacturers. He visits the first dealer in order to see and feel the product. Once he has guided himself around the showroom he looks around for a salesman; he has questions and would like to arrange a test drive. The salesman is, however, busy attending to another customer, and pays him no attention. Our customer is very likely to leave the dealership and go consider his alternative choice. If he gets better service there he is likely to buy.

Retailers often face this situation, where it is just not economically justifiable to have extra resources available "just in case" an extra customer requires help.

In my early career as a district sales manager for Peugeot, I used to swap territories for the day with other district sales managers, and we would "mystery shop" each others' dealers. We would carry cash on us so that we could award instant prizes to those that we felt offered exceptional service.

On one particular day I had visited five dealerships and been spectacularly unimpressed by the service I had received, and hence as I approached the sixth it took considerable will power to put myself in the situation once again. This last dealership for the day was a medium-sized operation in a provincial town.

I opened the door to the showroom and stepped inside. The solitary salesman on duty in the smallish display area was busy with a customer. Seated across the desk from each other, they were deep in conversation about the details of a deal.

I sighed privately and resolved to wait for a while to see what would happen. I meandered around the showroom in my role as a prospective purchaser and settled by a particular vehicle, reading the specification displayed on the windscreen.

The salesman appeared at my elbow with a warm smile of greeting.

"Hello, my name is John Brown. I'm just tied up at the moment, but

I shouldn't be more than five minutes. Are you able to wait? Can I get you a cup of coffee – we've just had a new machine delivered and it's really good."

Things were looking up. The aroma of fresh coffee filled the show-room and soon I had my own cup – not a plastic one but a nice, expensive-feeling cup and saucer. This was great. It takes a good five minutes for most people to drink a really hot cup of coffee. The salesman had effectively "parked" me, but in the process had given me a rich experience of great coffee. He went on to do a great job of qualifying me and identifying my needs. I had to hand over his cash prize quickly before I found myself buying a car.

> I HAD TO HAND OVER his cash prize quickly before I found myself buying a car.

Few organisations that have to deliver service are good at proactively managing the start of the waiting process and yet this is key to setting up the conditions for a successful sale.

KICKING THINGS OFF

A good queueing system should allow consumers to register their interest for service at the earliest possible moment. It can be observed empirically that queueing creates tension and stress – queuers are anxious to ensure that they do not miss their turn and that they "do the right thing at the right time." The most significant factor in lowering consumer stress is providing the means for the consumer to "check in" at the time of their arrival, thereby establishing their priority in the order of service. Provided that the queue management method then conveys feedback to the consumer that they are acknowledged to be in the right place at the right time, then all conditions are met to keep stress to a minimum. The consumer can then focus on other more positive distractions.

To give an example which most readers can relate to, Maister cites restaurant service as a classic illustration of this phenomenon; I adapt his example here:

Imagine that you have arrived at a popular and busy restaurant and you have a table booked for 8 p.m. The minutes are ticking by and you cannot attract anyone's attention to register your arrival, get a menu or order an aperitif. How do you feel?

Now, imagine the situation where although the restaurant is full and you will clearly be late in sitting down for your dinner, you and your party receive a courteous welcome from the restaurant manager, your coats are taken, you are sat in the bar, the drinks you order arrive promptly and you are left to peruse the menu. In the latter situation you have been professionally queue-managed. Your arrival has been acknowledged and in your mind service has therefore started. Although your transaction will be later than you expected you have been

> YOUR ARRIVAL has been acknowledged; service has started. You have been professionally queue-managed.

positively distracted by the arrival of drinks and the menus. The latter has the second bonus in that it will improve utilisation of table space for the restaurant – you will not occupy valuable minutes at the table choosing your meal.

Staff who do the right thing – make eye contact, acknowledge the customer, apologise for the wait (but only if there has actually been one) – make a big difference to how we as consumers feel about these situations.

THE F WORD

There is a further precondition to establishing acceptable wait times – fairness. The word "fair" crops up more often than any other in research into consumer attitudes to queueing. Provided that consumers feel that their turn for service is unequivocally reserved and that no one can "queue-jump" then they will be much more tolerant of waiting time.

There may be nothing worse than waiting in a long line in a bank for a counter with eight serving positions – but only two of them staffed. Actually that's not quite true. The one thing that's pretty much guaranteed to wind the tension up further is when a well-meaning member of the staff comes and "floor-walks," asking customers waiting at the middle or end of the line – all of whom have waited less time than the people at the front – if they are just paying in cheques or have some other simple transaction that doesn't necessarily need a teller. On more than one occasion I have seen customers at the front of the line react angrily to this approach and suggest that the member of staff get behind the counter and help serve the line faster.

> **NOTHING WORSE** than waiting in a long line for a counter with eight serving positions – but only two of them staffed.

The linear queue is seen by customers as patently fair because it stores waiting shoppers in the order of their arrival.

However this is not always the best way to allocate service. In certain circumstances it can be right to serve customers in an order which is other than first in, first out. Priority for service can be established in other ways than on the time of arrival and keeping each person's waiting time as short as possible, for instance in a hospital's emergency treatment department. In

PRIORITY FOR SERVICE can be established in other ways than the time of arrival.

such situations priority will go to those with most urgent need, irrespective of their arrival time. Hospitals will try to make sure that sufficient resources are available to ensure that no one will have to wait for an excessive length of time. Anyone attending an emergency department with a minor injury is preconditioned to expect a significant wait.

The waiting scenario for emergency departments still works because in this context "fair" means prioritising the treatment of someone who is more seriously ill than those with more minor ailments. In this situation the queue effectively become a series of queues with individuals categorised into, say, high, medium and low priority, with patients likely to be served in order of their being allocated into these three "notional queues."

There are thus circumstances where as the organisation providing the service you deliberately want to serve customers other than in the order they arrived.

SHORTEST PROCESSED FIRST

When I first came across the notion of "Shortest Processed First," in my mind it took on a magical quality, a kind of arithmetic sleight of hand.

I found myself explaining how it worked on a pristine whiteboard in the shiny new offices of a bank in the north of England. I had a room full of operations people and a highly paid consultant from a major consultancy practice who were advising the bank. I had better make this good.

I picked up the marker pen.

"At the moment, you serve all of your customers in the order of their arrival, what we call 'First In, First Out.'" I wrote FIFO as a heading on the board.

"I would like you to consider using an alternative methodology, which we call 'Shortest Processed First.'" I wrote SPF alongside FIFO.

"Now let's consider eight customers all of whom arrive in turn. We will call the first one who walks in A, the next one B and so on until we come through to the last one, H." I wrote A through H down the left-hand side of the board.

"And now, under the FIFO column we are going to record the time it took to serve each of those customers, in the order of their arrival." I wrote down a series of random service times between 0.5 and 8.2 minutes under FIFO and alongside each letter.

At the bottom of the column under FIFO, I added up the total service time for the eight customers.

"Now in this simple example, I will assume that there is only one person serving, and so the customer wait time will be the sum of the service times of the customers being served or waiting in front of them."

First In First Out (FIFO) Customers served in order of time of arrival		
Customer *by arrival order*	Service duration (mins)	Waiting time (mins)
A	5.3	0
B	8.2	5.3
C	2.1	13.5
D	0.5	15.6
E	3.1	16.1
F	4.6	19.2
G	2.2	23.8
H	1.3	26.0
Total service time	27.3	
Average service time	3.4	
Average waiting time		14.9

Average waiting time in a single-server single queue: FIFO

I then created a second column for "waiting time" and showed how I had worked this out.

Finally, at the bottom of the table, I calculated the average waiting time for our group of eight fictitious customers: 14.9 minutes.

"Now supposing that we had known in advance how long it would take for each customer transaction and instead of serving them in the order that they arrived we served the person who had the shortest transaction first and the next shortest and so on. What do you think the impact on waiting time would be?"

"Surely it has to be the same," someone piped up. "There are the same number of customers, with the same transactions, and only one person serving, so nothing will change."

I created a second column of figures under the SPF heading, reordering the customers according to the length of their transaction, shortest at the top, and then recalculated the average waiting time. Although the average service time was still of course 3.4 minutes per customer, the average waiting time had dropped from 14.9 to 6.8 minutes.

"Any questions?" I asked.

Stunned silence.

In the UK, our first practical application of SPF came out of our growing relationship with Argos. In the late 90s Argos's unique business model was in many ways a precursor to internet shopping. Millions of printed catalogues were distributed through their stores three or four times a year, allowing shoppers to browse their latest range and select items in the comfort of their homes. At the stores, customers would go to the browser bars, where they could again look at catalogues to confirm their purchase, fill in the stock code of the goods they had selected on a slip of paper, and go to a cash register to pay. From the cash register they would go with their receipt to a collection counter, where they would wait for their purchases to travel from the warehouse. Customers would line up at the collection counters in the order that they arrived from the cash registers. The goods arriving from the warehouse, however, almost never arrived in the same order as the customers. Size, weight and stock location were the main determinants of getting goods to counter. And so the staff would end up having to wave items in the air or shout out to customers at the back of the line.

Shortest Processed First (SPF) Customers served in order of service duration		
Customer *reordered*	Service duration (mins)	Waiting time (mins)
D	0.5	0
H	1.3	0.5
C	2.1	1.8
G	2.2	3.9
E	3.1	6.1
F	4.6	9.2
A	5.3	13.8
B	8.2	19.1
Total service time	27.3	
Average service time	3.4	
Average waiting time		6.8

Average waiting time in a single-server single queue: SPF

This just about worked throughout most of year when most customers bought one or two items. During the seasonal trading peak – roughly October to the end of January – when something like two-thirds of the trade took place, it was a different story. Customers would wait in a crowd, order having largely broken

CUSTOMERS WOULD wait in a crowd, order having largely broken down.

down. Anyone with a walking stick or a pushchair would try to wait at the edge. People's good humour would wear thin in the week before

Christmas. The staff tried hard to make it as good as possible. At one stage Argos decided to allocate extra staff to the stores to try to get people served quicker and eliminate the queues, but this really didn't help. With more people behind the counter yelling out and moving things around, the only certain result was that store operating costs went up; no one got served any faster.

What was needed was a new approach.

We first proposed keeping customers away from the collection counters, only calling them forward once their goods arrived there. This would certainly have created a much more orderly and pleasant environment, but everyone was concerned that it might prove too slow in practice.

We suddenly realised that we had what we needed for "Shortest Processed First." In each store, Argos held a database of where each item was held in the warehouse at the back of the sales floor. From this, we could calculate how long it would take to get each item to the collection counters – and therefore the estimated time of collection. If the estimates proved accurate then customers would be summoned just as their goods arrived there, creating a smooth flow.

What made this possible was our ability to create a relationship in the customers' minds between the number of items on their order and the time it would take to assemble it. It felt like common sense to them that an order that had more items in it would take longer to put together, and hence necessitate a longer wait.

We produced a prototype system that generated a unique order number and collection time for each customer, which could be given to them along with their receipt at payment. Monitors placed around the store would show the progress of each order number. As the collection time arrived a voice would announce "Order Number 163, please go to your collection point," supported by the same message appearing on the screen.

Staff were on hand in the first weeks of the new system to help customers through their initial visit. The customers quickly absorbed the new process and were very happy with the result. As the weeks went by, a steady stream of new customers were coming into the store to make purchases for the first time in many years. Further investigation showed that these new customers had been referred by recent users of the new system.

The in-store research that Argos's board commissioned asking customers what they thought of the new system produced such an amazing result that the company in question was obliged to repeat the exercise to prove it was accurate.

Incredibly over 85% of customers felt their shopping experience had materially improved, and 77% were surprised how short the wait was.

Argos announced their Christmas trading results in February and made a direct connection between their in-store investment in "queue management" and sales growth. The story made the front page of the Financial Times. It was my best Christmas present ever. Our phones glowed cherry red for a week.

MAKING A PROMISE – AND KEEPING IT

A minute left hanging on the end of a telephone can feel like an hour. In the same way six minutes spent standing in line can pass really quickly or feel like purgatory. It is possible to "bend" shoppers' perception of passing time by up to half, so that a six-minute wait feels like three. Customers who are on edge about whether they will be served in turn are stressed and time-conscious. Fair service allocation and being seen to be trying are key to managing customers' expectations.

> **HOW LONG will it be?**
> **– I'm not sure but we**
> **will get back to you.**

There are few things worse than waiting for something and not knowing how long you will be waiting for. I have seen customers arrive at the bank to enquire at the help desk – "I would like to see someone about a mortgage, please" – only to be asked to take a seat in a waiting area.

"How long will it be?"

"I'm not sure but we will get to you as soon as we can."

I watched the customer go back to the help desk several times only to be sent back to his seat each time. An hour and 40 minutes – that's how long he waited. Was he in the right frame of mind to be sold a product at the end of this? I doubt it.

"Positive feedback" means keeping people updated with whatever information that you have about the queue length and wait time. Such updates should be honest and forthright. Organisations that withhold information in the interests of not displeasing us pay the penalty in the long run.

Airlines are particularly poor at managing this situation. Rather than telling us upfront what is likely to happen, they seem to spin out the process with as little information as possible at each stage. I found myself at Edinburgh airport one evening just before Christmas. It had been a long day, as I had flown up from London in the early morning, and after a series of meetings that had lasted most of the day, was only now checking in for my flight home. There had been snow and ice in the forecast all day and the weather had deteriorated throughout the long, grey afternoon. No one was particularly surprised that our flight was delayed, initially. However, as the evening wore on, things became increasingly tense. A pattern emerged. As each promised departure time expired, a new announcement would be made delaying us for another hour. As soon as each announcement was made frustrated passengers would rush to the desk to ask the staff for more information – which they declined to give. All we could do as hapless victims was to wait it out to see what transpired.

AS EACH promised departure time expired, a new announcement would be made delaying us for another hour.

The original scheduled departure time was 7 p.m.; by 10.45 p.m., having seen four promised departure times pass us by, the coup de grace was delivered. A final announcement told us that not only was the flight now cancelled, the ticket office was closed, and there would be no point contacting the airline through their website or by telephone as all flights the next day were fully booked. During the hours between our initial promised departure time and this final announcement, all of the staff had discreetly drifted away, leaving no one for us to buttonhole about our situation. Interestingly only this airline was so badly affected – all the others appeared to have managed to keep their planes flying. I don't believe in conspiracy theories but that night felt a lot like a stitch-up. No one from the airline at any time expressed remorse or apologised for the situation that we found ourselves in. That was it, we were on our own.

I have rarely felt so let down and angry. Wouldn't it have been more honest to explain much earlier that the weather was closing in and the most likely outcome was going to be a cancelled flight? I take the cynical view that the airline in question was more concerned about preserving revenue – by keeping all the passengers on hand just in case they could fly their plane – than they were about long-term customer relationships.

One of the big no-nos when you have customers waiting is to make a promise and break it. If you believe the waiting time is going to be nine minutes, promise ten, not eight; that way, people are pleasantly surprised when they are served a little quicker than they were prepared to wait. If you know that your waiting promise is going to be broken, you should intervene before this happens, not after.

> ONE OF THE big no-nos when you have customers waiting is to make a promise and break it.

So how should the airline have handled my situation? The first thing they could have done was to warn passengers at check-in that there was a possibility of a flight delay due to expected weather deterioration. Given that boarding normally takes place some minutes before take-off, they should have made an announcement and updated their screens as soon as they knew that circumstances had changed and not waited for the scheduled departure time to expire. As soon as cancellation became a possibility they should have said so. At the same time they should have reminded passengers of their cancellation policy and made members of staff available to answer questions and offer assistance. Customers would, I'm sure, still have got agitated but this would have been minimised by professional handling, as compared to the act of cowardice that I witnessed that night.

When the regular processes break down, human intervention is critical to brand integrity. Intelligent, well-trained staff can minimise the damage that such failures cause and can even turn the situation to a positive outcome.

RELEVANT DISTRACTION

Unoccupied time always feels longer than when you are busy with something. If we go back to Maister's restaurant example a great way of entertaining would-be diners until their table is available is with a menu. For these diners the evening has started. They can savour the descriptions of each dish and conjure up pictures and tastes in their heads. They can talk to one other and compare notes – "What are you going to have?" – and compare the merits of the different main courses. When handled well, waiting becomes anticipation, a pleasurable part of the dining experience. Great restaurants know how to pace their patrons through this process, allowing enough time for it to be enjoyable but not so much that it becomes over-extended. It's quite common these days to be given a pager on arrival and sent to the bar to get a drink and wait. This is fine but it does nothing to start to engage the diner with the meal that they are about to have. Even the most humble chain restaurant would see a benefit from handing out menus along with those pagers.

In his book, *The Mechanism of the Mind*, Edward De Bono relates a story which is often quoted in queue management circles. The version that I heard goes as follows. In the 1930s, a new skyscraper office block in New York had just been completed. The contemporary design included the latest elevators specified to move people around the building as quickly as possible. However, within a few months the building's owners were receiving complaints from their tenants that their employees and guests were being delayed by the "slow elevators." Long queues would form in the lobbies of each floor and frustrated staff would arrive at their desks to start their working day in a bad mood. The owners wanted to know who was at fault. Had the architects specified the wrong type of elevator? Had the manufacturer delivered the wrong equipment? Had the builders installed the equipment wrongly? The owners hired an independent consultant to examine the situation. He made timings of the process, looked at the design of the elevators, and reached his conclusion. He was called in to pronounce his verdict. He concluded that there was no practical way to improve the performance of the elevators and that the building was a victim of its own success, with more visitors than had been originally planned. However, he surprised the owners with a simple plan by which he believed they could reduce and possibly eliminate the complaints from people waiting in the lobby.

> **UNOCCUPIED TIME always feels longer than when you are busy with something.**

"It's very simple," he said. "If we install large mirrors in each lobby, people will be so busy looking at themselves that they will be distracted from how long they are waiting for the elevator."

The legend goes that it worked and the complaints were all but eliminated.

IN-STORE DIGITAL MEDIA

Intelligent use of digital media in store can play a big part in helping to manage shoppers' perception of waiting time – but only if it is done well. A few recycled TV ads playing on a large-format screen just won't cut the mustard.

Visual noise competes for our attention constantly. The more messages that you are confronted with, the less you take in. Therefore a carefully considered in-store media strategy limits messages to ensure that shoppers can achieve their primary function in store, and discreetly presents them with appropriate messages at key parts of their store journey.

From our observations, about 85% of customers who stand in a linear queue look at the "Cashier Number Three Please" screen. When we started upgrading those screens to LCD so that we could show media, we created a very interesting opportunity.

Ambient media screens – the ones scattered throughout the store – give customers no compelling reason to look at them. But when content was moved from the ambient screens to the screen at the head of the queue, information-recall rates went up by a factor of ten. It is vital, though, that the queueing information is on the same screen; if it's just a second screen that sits alongside the queue management system, the effect is lost.

Content is king in such situations. One retailer created their in-store content through the same advertising agency who produced their TV ads. Unfortunately the agency was unaware of just how quickly the queue moved. Before they were called, shoppers only ever saw the beginning, middle or end of the witty and clever content that had been created just for them. Expensive and pointless.

And what happens if customers get hooked on watching a programme that turns out to be longer than their wait time for service? They drag out their journey to the counter in order to watch an extra minute or two of their favourite programme. Meanwhile the member of staff who is waiting to serve them has to do just that – wait. Productivity is reduced, fewer customers get served.

> IF IT'S JUST a second screen that sits alongside the queue management system, the effect is lost.

The best material for in-store media is a mix of bite-sized, quick-to-process brand information and entertainment. Trivia is some of the best stuff. "Did you knows" are very effective – for instance "Did you know that polar bears are left-handed?" It's not going to change anyone's life, but a smile is a valuable gift.

A more sophisticated approach is possible for virtual queues. Data from individual customers' check-ins can be used to dynamically shape the media content playing on the screens, targetting their specific interests while they are in the store.

Most marketing departments' idea of in-store messages, however, still remains at the level of producing posters which are shipped to each location, where staff are tasked to fix them to walls at a time to tie in with

regional or national campaign activity. The cost of in-store "paper promotional materials" can be very high. Datamonitor estimates that European
banks spend €1.67 billion annually on brochures and paper advertising
materials for in-store use.[5] Yet much of this expense is wasted. For many
store chains, compliance – that is, the extent to which posters end up at
the intended place at the intended time – can be as low as 50%.

Digital media does not have this problem. Content generated cen-
trally can be scheduled to appear at exactly the right times in exactly the
right stores. Content can be delivered locally which dovetails into other
local media messages or campaigns and the tastes of local audiences.

But the challenge of producing so much content can be daunting. It's
like running your own TV channel. Not for the faint hearted and better
not to start than to give up. Busi-
nesses who deploy in-store media
must have a long-term commitment – beyond mere investment in
infrastructure – to ensure that there
is always something interesting and
relevant for customers to look at.

**I ONCE SPENT an afternoon
watching the TV channel at
one branch, counting how
many of its competitors'
ads were played!**

But very few customer-facing organisations have risen to this challenge.

It is depressing to see so many screens in stores and bank branches
turned off or showing the same old content. Worse still some organisations
have turned over the screens to commercial TV stations in the interests
of giving their customers something to watch. I once spent an afternoon
watching the TV channel at one particular bank, counting how many of
its competitors' ads were played!

IT'S ALL IN THE PERCEPTION

One of the hardest things for retailers who are new to this subject to get their heads around is the idea that queue management is all about managing shoppers' perceptions; how long it takes to get served is only one component of perception.

Maister, in his paper, "The Psychology of Waiting Lines," explained it through a simple, powerful formula:

$$S = P - E$$

where S is satisfaction, P is perception and E is expectation.

In other words, customers are satisfied when the perceived service exceeds their expectations. And if their perception of the event was much better than they expected, they will tell all of their friends and come back and buy more.

09

MAKING
LEAN SERVICE
DELIVERY A REALITY

I HAVE SEEN MANY ORGANISATIONS WHO, after receiving bad scores from their customers for queue management, make the decision to increase their investment in staff hours – only to see their poor scores persist, or indeed worsen. What they fail to understand are the diminishing returns of adding extra resource at the margin.

With one speciality retailer we worked with, their own research showed deep customer dissatisfaction with waiting times in store, despite the fact that on average customers waited for less than three minutes. Their first attempt at cracking this problem was to increase staff hours by some 25% – adding substantially to their overheads – in the expectation that they could significantly reduce customer wait times and consequently increase satisfaction. In reality the opposite happened. New temporary staff were drafted in over their trading peak. Despite receiving training, the new staff members were less familiar with systems and procedures than regular staff and slowed things down to a disastrous degree. Costs went up, customer wait times increased to over four minutes, and customer dissatisfaction rocketed.

We designed a new process for service allocation which was more orderly and less stressful. By working with the stores and observing customer–staff interaction, we mapped each stage of the customer journey on a "brown paper" – literally a single sheet of brown paper large enough to

104

cover a boardroom table and to map each event. This allowed us to develop a system to "check customers in" and call them for service in the most efficient way. With the new model, we reduced staff hours by 30% from the original model – re-allocating surplus staff into support functions – and increased customer wait time to over seven minutes. Overnight, customer satisfaction virtually doubled. Absolute speed of service is much less important to customers than fairness and order.

THE NUMBERS AND THE PSYCHOLOGY

We have seen that psychology – the way people feel about the place and the process they are in – is a big part of the experience they will carry away from a store visit. The mathematics of service provision – how many staff are available to serve, how many customers are waiting, how long transactions take – are

ABSOLUTE SPEED of service is much less important than fairness and order.

only components of the overall perception that is created. However, they have big implications for the organisation that is providing the service.

The numbers are important because organisations that provide service to consumers invest billions in delivering that service. Efficiency gains here lead to bottom-line savings. A great queue management strategy, properly executed, can not only deliver a better customer experience but save money at the same time, delivering a return on investment in an outrageously short period. Almost all of the projects that I have witnessed in the last fifteen years have seen this result.

WHAT'S THE RIGHT NUMBER OF REGISTERS?

A great illustration of lean service delivery – improving service while freeing up resource – comes from a project I carried out with John Lewis, looking at their "Back to School" department.

John Lewis is an unusual chain of department stores in that they are a privately held company, owned and operated by their "partners," the staff who work in the organisation. They pride themselves on offering high levels of service and great value with their trading philosophy "Never knowingly undersold."

My relationship with John Lewis had begun in early 2005 with my helping them to develop their thinking around cash-taking and to plan new store layouts. By moving to linear cash-taking and paying close attention to shoppers' lines of sight and way-finding in store, we had reduced the number of registers in use, hence freeing up partners to move out from the registers onto the shop floor, enhancing customer service.

> WE REDUCED the number of registers in use, freeing up partners to move around.

With John Lewis I acted as an "expert witness." The partnership model made a great difference to the atmosphere in those meetings, as compared to more conventional management structures in other retailers I had worked with. I found a professional, highly motivated management team who built consensus in an open, non-political way, and with a genuine desire to assimilate best practice and increase the power of their business model.

CHILDREN'S SHOES:
SAVING MONEY WHILE IMPROVING SERVICE

Perhaps that was just as well, considering the next challenge they threw at me. Once we had completed re-designing the stores for cash-taking, I was asked to consider the issues around "Back to School," and specifically the children's shoe department.

Children grow fast; so do their feet. This means frequent return trips by parents to shoe retailers to acquire new footwear. The sizing of children's feet and the fitting of shoes is something of a "black art": gauges are used in store to find the size in terms of length and width fitting, but then the actual fit of a shoe in the chosen style needs to be checked on the child's foot, and in some cases a larger or smaller size is needed in order to get a good comfortable fit – and room for some future growth. Partners are trained in this role for which they require the knowledge of a seller, the patience of a saint, and the entertainment skills of Coco the Clown in order to keep a child's attention through the necessary process.

Given that kids' shoes aren't cheap, parents tend to leave it until the last possible weekend before school starts; and then inevitably they all try to shop at the same time. Parents could wait as long as two-and-a-half hours to get service. This would be difficult enough to manage if it was just adults waiting but when a typical shopping group would involve one or two harassed parents and two children under eight it became very difficult. Small children who haven't been socialised into the niceties of queueing and prefer to run around screaming don't help a hard-pressed department trying to get everyone served as quickly as possible.

Normal operations and coping strategies

John Lewis called me in to review the way these extreme seasonal peaks could be handled. In order to do so, I visited a selection of stores across the country, talking to partners to get their views and skulking in the corners of departments discreetly observing what transpired.

Most of the stores, during the normal course of business, used a simple "Take a Ticket" system. At peak trading times, however, this was insufficient to maintain order in the process. (All the larger stores had, space allowing, child-friendly areas with TV and toys to try to keep waiting children entertained and offer some respite to hard-pressed parent and partners). At peak periods the "Take a Ticket" system would be abandoned in favour of a number of different coping strategies:

Some stores issued pagers to parents arriving in the department. The partner who was acting as the "service allocator" would take down the family name on a chart, give a rough estimate of waiting time, and issue a pager. Families could then roam free around the store, or indeed the shopping centre, until summoned back by the buzzing pager to take their turn at getting served. However, many of the stores were located in large shopping malls, in which there would be a significant number of "dead spots" where the pager simply would not pick up the radio signal.

> THE SIZING of children's feet and the fitting of shoes is something of a "black art."

Some stores put in a similar system using customers' mobile phones. However, where there was either no mobile phone coverage or busy networks, the text message sent by the store summoning the customer back would not get through in a timely fashion – negating the process.

Other stores simply booked an appointment slot for later in the day, effectively rescheduling demand into a time slot where they believed that they would have capacity.

The effect of these coping strategies on customer behaviour was interesting and understandable. Even the most faithful John Lewis customers became "promiscuous shoppers." Having accepted a pager from the store they would leave the department, leave the store, travel through the mall and enter a competitor's store where they would take a ticket and wait. Whoever called them for service first would get the sale.

> **EVEN THE MOST FAITHFUL customers became "promiscuous shoppers."**

That is provided that they had stock available in the requisite size. The peak was so marked that it was difficult to keep sufficient stock of all sizes and all styles on hand, and, together with a lack of good demographic data in the industry indexing age to foot size, stock levels became something of a guessing game for purchasing departments.

In store John Lewis had a further strand to their strategy to serve customers faster. Typically around eight partners per store were trained to assess children's foot sizes and would regularly work the department; in addition, a significant number of partners who normally worked in other departments were also trained in this and were always available to be summoned at short notice to work alongside the regular fitters. The analysis showed that while this was a well-intentioned strategy, it was a misguided one.

It takes a well-trained fitter around 12 minutes to assess a child's foot size, retrieve stock from the warehouse area and carry out a trial fitting. Their finely honed diplomacy skills in working with the child and their confidence in using the foot gauge, both built on regular use, contributed to their speedy service. The irregular troops – the ones who undertook this work occasionally – were much slower, taking about 50% longer to accomplish the same task. Compounded by the limited size of the departments – most could accommodate no more than ten family groups at a time – this influx of well-intentioned but slower troops was slowing the process down and clogging up the available space.

> **THE IRREGULAR TROOPS took 50% longer to accomplish the same task.**

A different strategy was needed.

First we examined the manual sheets that partners used to record customer requests for service. By comparing these with the process capability of the most effective partners, we were able to build a model of the maximum throughput that could be achieved in each department.

Our strategy was to focus on a "lean process" – using the highly trained and well-practised team of regular operators in the department, and removing all blockers to their speed of service. By doing so, we could leverage much higher throughput.

For this to work, however, we needed to keep all aspects of the department lean, and that included not having large numbers of stressed parents hanging around for their turn. But at the same time we didn't want sales opportunities leaking away to competitors because we were pushing customer service times back. How could we solve this conundrum?

It was clear to me that we would need to offer arriving customers an appointment with a time delay against it, allowing us to spread the peaks and troughs of demand across our flat-capacity serving machine. This appointment time would be set by an algorithm in our software which would examine available serving capacity, current performance levels, and demand already scheduled.

However, if the time interval between arrival and serving time was too small, customers would simply hang around in the department until their appointment time, and chaos would ensue. Yet if the service time was too long then shoppers would have time to leave the store and "behave promiscuously" with the opposition.

We devised a formula where every appointment would carry a time delay of at least fifteen minutes. If, however, the calculated time delay worked out to be more than 40 minutes we would intervene to keep the customer in the store in some other way. The idea behind these two time points was inspired by Paco Underhill. Underhill had stated that the longer happy and relaxed customers stay in store, the more they shop – and so we hoped that we might see some incremental sales as evidence that the system was working well. By hitting on these two "end stops" we hoped that it would give most customers the time and the motivation to move away from the department and browse surrounding areas but insufficient time to leave the store.

Offer and confirm

The system we eventually implemented worked like this. Customers arriving at the department would first check in at an electronic terminal. Initially we had planned for a partner to "host" this terminal, but the design that we created turned out to be so user-friendly that customers quickly took to using it for themselves.

At check-in the customer was asked to confirm how many children required fitting, their ages and sex. This allowed us to capture demographic data which could be matched up with size data at the end of the transaction and which would in turn help the purchasing department ensure future stock availability of the right size-to-age profile.

The customer would then be offered the earliest available time slot. If they accepted this appointment, a "service receipt" would be printed confirming the service that they had requested and the time of the appointment. We have found that presenting the customer with an estimated wait time at check-in and then offering them the option to accept or decline makes the process much stickier – after all they have been given the choice and opportunity to walk away and not taken it. Once they have accepted the wait time and have a physical "service promise" in their hands, almost all customers wait the full time to service. And in this mode they do what comes naturally: they shop, they browse, they consider rich media messages that are presented to them (but only if the content is relevant and particularly where there is queueing

> THE OFFER-AND-CONFIRM process effectively resets the customer's expectations around the transaction.

information on the screen). Most customers are surprised at how short the projected wait time is. I believe that this "offer and confirm" process effectively resets the customer's expectations around the transaction.

The software algorithm then takes over the process, ensuring that the customer is called at or slightly before the appointed time, and, if for some reason this is no longer possible, alerts staff in a timely manner, allowing them to intervene with the customer before the promised wait time has expired. This whole service allocation process addresses Meister's $S = P - E$ equation by resetting expectations with the customer's active complicity, and then ensuring that the mathematical part of P, the wait time, is effectively managed.

On the service side, each member of the fitting team would "make themselves available" to the system via a two-way pager that allowed them to receive service requests and send acknowledgements. An allocated supervisor would receive additional information through his pager, to monitor the status of the "service engine" and ensure that the process was being optimised. As the service history database compiled its history of transactions, the algorithm, buried within the software, would improve its waiting-time forecast.

Results

We installed this new system at the John Lewis store in Southampton – to an enthusiastic welcome. Whereas previously customers would have had to wait up to two-and-a-half hours, with the new system in place almost all customers were seen within 40 minutes. The children's shoe department was transformed. No more harassed parents coping with overwrought children. The previous scenes of back-to-school chaos were replaced by a calm, efficient environment which put the competition to shame. We were also able to save a valuable partner's time too – there was no longer any need for a "service allocator" in the department, thus liberating a partner for more constructive work. The improvement in efficiency, together with the invaluable data generated around sales conversion and sizing, made this a very effective tool for superior service delivery. It wasn't long before we were talking about putting the system across other busy stores in the chain.

Commenting on the impact of the deployment, the manager for selling services, responsible for the project for John Lewis, said, "This roll-out has helped us gain a real competitive edge in children's footwear and has helped improve the customer experience at the same time. The team at Qmatic have developed and deployed a solution that made an immediate impact and in the long term, the data we capture will help us refine our range and assortment planning process in this area."

> **ALL CUSTOMERS were seen within 40 minutes. The department was transformed.**

A BUSINESS WITHOUT QUEUES?

Many of the service organisations I've worked with over the years tell me, "I want to eliminate queues in my stores." This is the bold cry I hear at the start of many meetings on this subject. If that's what you think too, forget it – it's never going to happen.

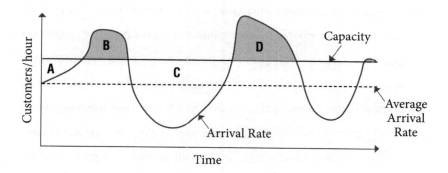

Customer arrivals over time

The graph above explains the dilemma faced by managers who must schedule their staff to try to match customer demand for service while managing their operating costs as efficiently as possible. The manager must forecast the number of staff he makes available and agree on it with head office. To do this he uses the average customer arrival rate (dotted line) and then adds a little to it so he has some spare capacity built into his model (solid line). But because each customer arrival is inherently unpredictable, actual arrivals are much more volatile than the average line would suggest. The wavy line shows this. Where the arrival rate exceeds the capacity line (sections B and D), there will be customers waiting for service, and a queue will form. Where the store has excess capacity (sections A & C), there will be staff waiting to serve customers, and valuable hours of serving time being wasted.

The store has a strategic decision to make. Is operating cost more important than customer service? If it is then they will move the capacity line down and make customers wait longer; this will lower the average cost per transaction of delivering service for the store chain. On the other hand, if stores decide that service times are more important to their brand proposition than cost or if they know that because of the nature of their business customers will be less tolerant of waiting times, they will move the capacity line up, ensuring that fewer customers have to wait, but increasing the cost of their operation and risking more times when they will have staff standing idle.

> THE STORE HAS a strategic decision to make: Is operating cost more important than customer service?

This dilemma can be resolved through lean queue management. By making wait times more acceptable, and by organising service allocation systems – "serving engines," which are as efficient as possible in converting serving hours to satisfied customers – they can help to lower costs and reduce waste in the process.

A paper by Professor Edward Anderson (from whom this diagram is borrowed), "A Note on Managing Waiting Lines," provides more detail on the mathematical basis for this.[6] It demonstrates the relationship between service capacity, server utilisation and the distribution of service times and arrival rates:

- If all servers are constantly busy, the queue quickly exceeds acceptable levels.
- The "lumpier" the arrival rate, the longer the queue. So in smaller stores with lighter traffic – where arrival rate is less predictable – the waits are likely to be longer.

- The more the staff keep their service times consistent, the shorter the wait customers experience.
- There is a limit to the number of servers it makes sense to have in a store, as at some point the cost of an additional server will not be repaid by shorter wait times for customers.

Not everyone understands that customer waiting time and queues are an arithmetic certainty of service delivery. In the real world, even when you have extra staff available just in case demand builds up, queues will occur. It's in the nature of customer arrivals that shoppers arrive in bunches and not in a steady flow.

SIGNS OF GOOD HEALTH

Well-planned and well-managed queues are a healthy thing. They indicate a vibrant business which is successfully controlling the cost of delivering service to its customers and at the same time managing shoppers' perceptions of their wait. Whether there are only two people waiting or 42, the right mathematical methodology has been used to determine how to serve customers as efficiently as possible and how to

> **WELL-PLANNED and well-managed queues are a healthy thing.**

allocate service fairly. You can see the impact of a well-managed queue on the faces of the customers and servers. They are relaxed, unstressed. Waiting customers look around them and take an interest in merchandise. The store receives fewer complaints and suffers lower staff absenteeism. Conversely

117

a business without queues is either overmanned or lacking customers – or worse, both.

In practice almost all service-delivery organisations today have the computer software to manage the cost of face-to-face service provision. These programmes schedule work by means of a staffing roster – planned to the hour, and implemented across the retailer's chain – taking into account the required tasks to operate each store, and attempting to meet customer demand through peak trading hours. Such programmes, however, take a formulaic approach to assessing staff hours in relation to the time each task takes and the number of times the task will occur. Two weaknesses are inherent:

The first is that the effectiveness of the programme depends critically upon an accurate assessment of customer demand within the planning period that is being forecast. This is, however, problematic in itself, in terms of getting at accurate historical data and applying such data as a predictor of future demand levels.

Secondly such systems can make no assessment of the efficiency of the "service engine" as it is established within the organisation. They simply take data which is based on the way the organisation is currently doing things and reflect this through as required hours for the planning period.

DATA DRIVES INSIGHT

Customer-arrivals data plays a key role in establishing a framework for service. Provided we don't cut it too finely and look at long-enough time intervals, to be statistically robust, it can give us a general sense of the average demand level. There are many ways this data is collected:

1. Virtual queue management systems record the moment the customer checks in and can also log each stage of the service process: when the customer is called for service, when the transaction starts, and when it concludes. This data lets organisations see how well they perform in practice. It also provides the data to allow real-time intervention when things go wrong.

2. Mobile phones are increasingly being used in queue management processes, as networks become more robust and can be relied upon to deliver timely signals within customer premises. The check-in process will in future be integrated with an online booking facility, and thus a picture of the whole experience can be compiled detailing the wait times at each stage and the service time as it was delivered. This will help the service delivery organisation to "tune" its serving engine to ensure that it maps exactly onto its brand proposition.

3. In stores with linear queues – or where there is for any reason no means of time-stamping the point at which the customer first requires service – customer numbers may be estimated through the use of sensors. It must be noted, though, that this data has generally been used more in the assessment of sales penetration (how many customers entered the store versus how many customer bought something) than for scheduling service capacity.

4. Digital camera technology is being used more and more as well. Intelligent software can track shoppers through the store, to see what they look at and where they stand. It can also recognise, say, three people

walking close together as a group shopping together rather than as individual shoppers; it can even, with increasing levels of accuracy, identify the gender of shoppers. This type of data generates insights around the whole customer experience and the way we interact with stores.

We have already seen that process capability data can be generated by the queue management system and this will map exactly how the serving engine responds under the load of variable customer demand. Data will automatically include the effects of service rates initially slowing when an additional server is added and any quirks of the system caused by process issues like the one I discussed earlier in relation to a carousel of paper forms. This data can be used to understand the "as is" of the serving engine, to measure performance and find ways to continuously improve it. By relating the process data to customer arrivals data gleaned from any available source it is possible to map customer waiting times and see how well the store responded to instantaneous demand for service.

> THE DATA collected can be used to understand the "as is" of the serving engine.

CUSTOMER FLOW MANAGEMENT

This way of thinking about queue management was pioneered by Qmatic. The company invented the term "customer flow management" (CFM) to describe customers' journey on their mission for service – from appointment-setting through service delivery – and all of the associated management information around each stage.

Built on over 30 years of global experience, CFM provides a unique data set – unobtainable from any other source – delivering a profound understanding of the metrics associated with customer demand, service supply and the waiting experience. This allows service organisations to dramatically improve throughput and costs, and continuously refine their offering. What gets measured gets improved.

The right strategy, which has

- a framework for an appropriate level of lean service delivery,
- the flexibility to be responsive to demand,
- the means by which service can be allocated fairly, and
- the know-how to proactively manage waiting customers' experience,

gives organisations that crucial competitive advantage – the ability to deliver great service at an affordable price.

10

THE
UNDERCOVER
SHOPPER

I HAVE LEARNED most of what I know about queueing by standing around in retail stores, banks, airports and other waiting environments, watching staff and customers. As I watched I would note down ideas, and then seek ways to substantiate them through data from wider sources. This has given me invaluable insight into behaviour and consequences. In all the dialogue that I have had with senior retailers and bankers, there is nothing more powerful than being able to describe to them, through the conviction of first-hand observation at the "queueing coal face," what if feels like to be a customer in their environment.

A TALENT FOR SKULKING

In this role there are two attributes that you need more than any other. The first is to be able to observe things meticulously and discreetly note them down. We human beings are quite transparent individuals. You can read an awful lot about how we are feeling in our faces and our body language. By watching these things I have been able to record situations where shoppers have been at their best and their worst in waiting situations.

The second skill required is the ability to become invisible.

I have learned that invisibility is an art not a science. No magic cloaks or spells are required. All that's needed is the ability to blend in, to assimilate the characteristics of the environment that you are in. The most common sight in a retail store is a shopper – so be a shopper.

On one occasion I was doing some work for an Irish bank in Dublin with two colleagues. We had been asked by their head office to carry out observations in several of their branches. Our team of three was accompanied into the branch by the project manager, who went off to look for the branch manager to tell him

> **"YOU'VE GOT TWO GUYS out there observing the branch, haven't you?"**

what was going on while we settled ourselves in. The branch manager was ready for his colleague when he arrived into his office.

"You've got two guys out there observing the branch, haven't you?"

"No," said the project manager. "I've got three!"

While the other two (mere amateurs!) had marched into the branch and "assumed position" in the corners of the foyer, I had slowed my walking pace and sauntered across to a waiting area where I could sit quietly and look around the branch while appearing to be staring into space, occasionally making a discreet note in the small book I had with me.

The quality of invisibility is important in ensuring that staff and customers' behaviour is not affected by the feeling that they are being watched. I know of one market research company that issues volunteer customers with special glasses before they enter a retail space. These glasses are able to record everything that the customer looks at inside the branch, but it would be naive to believe that this very act doesn't bias the result it's trying to record.

LEARNING TO BE INVISIBLE

The key characteristics of invisibility are dress and body language. If you are imagining me dressed in black and hiding behind a rack of greetings cards you would be completely wrong. Too smart and you look like staff and will be asked questions by members of the public; too scruffy and you are liable to be shown out. The trick is to look as "normal" as possible. Dress in the same mode as the store's usual customers; don't stand out.

Next is behaviour. I like this – it's a little like being a spy. Give yourself a mission before you enter the store. Think it through. There are two reasons for this. The first is that you will look more purposeful and will be less likely to be tackled by the staff; and second, if you are asked if you need help then you will have a cover story. Move slowly, no sudden gestures; stand near racks of product or brochures and hold your head as if you are looking at them, while actually moving just your eyes to observe what's going on around you. Find a chair and sit down, look slightly impatient and keep looking at your watch – in this one your cover story is that you are waiting for a friend who is currently being served.

> **MOVE SLOWLY, no sudden gestures, stand near racks of products or brochures...**

An in-store mission furthermore gives me a framework with which to judge how I feel about a store. If I was considering a bookshop and my mission was to buy a couple of good reads for a journey, I might think about some of the following attributes:

1. Lighting is probably quite important. For instance it might be desirable to have relatively low background light levels to create a relaxed

browsing atmosphere, but with localised areas of brighter lighting to allow shoppers to read titles on the shelves and to sit at comfy chairs and read a few pages.

2. Store navigation would be quite important as well, to allow people to home in on a subject area.

3. Book recommendations by staff would help introduce customers to books they might not otherwise have looked at, and at the same time add to the character and brand of the store.

Usually when I undertake undercover shopping I am doing so with the knowledge of the staff, but occasionally I am truly undercover. On these occasions it's very important to act natural and stay inconspicuous. My personal record so far has been to spend two hours in a small bank branch without being challenged by a member of the staff. This was an extraordinary and unexpected result.

Generally in these situations I like to observe the store through the build-up to and climb-down from a peak trading period. It can be very informative to see how things work not just when the store is busy but also when it's quiet, and also how and when the staff react to increases and decreases in traffic. What triggers do they use to increase staff levels on the shop floor as traffic increases? Are supervisors marshalling staff effectively?

The process of undercover shopping is as much about your own experience as it is about observing those of others. Constantly mapping your own feelings and comparing those with the body language and facial expression of the shoppers around you helps you to translate their feelings into words.

Recording the way processes work in reality is a key part of this. Far too many service organisations don't examine the actual events that occur closely enough. They rely on a theoretical approach, which may not reflect the working practices that are used in the real world. A consequence of this is that they almost certainly don't know how long it takes to serve a real customer in the store environment, and all of their calculations on work scheduling and productivity are off. That's why seeing it for yourself, recording how long each process takes and then perhaps subsequently interviewing staff and customers in order to gain a fuller picture are all vital stages in understanding what's required to get customers served. Only when you have an accurate record of what currently happens can you start to consider how it might be improved.

> **FAR TOO MANY service organisations don't examine the actual events closely enough. They rely on a theoretical approach.**

THREE TYPES OF CUSTOMERS

One of the biggest challenges facing staff and management is figuring out how many people will want to access service in their stores. We have already seen how unpredictable arrivals are, but there is a further difficulty: Not all of us go into a store to buy something today.

I have discovered through years of observation that there are three types of shoppers in a store at any given point in time. It is impossible to distinguish between them with the naked eye. If you ask a member of any

128

of the three groups whether they would like help before they are ready you will get the same reply – "I'm just looking."

But if you waited for them to ask for help, you may still be waiting when they leave the store without having spoken to anyone and you will never know whether a timely question would have facilitated a sale.

Let's take a closer look at the three groups and then discuss the contact strategy for each of them:

Today's buyers

The first group are our potential buyers today. They can number as few as 10% of the shoppers in store and they don't wear a special hat proclaiming "I am a buyer." Approach them too early and you may scare them off; approach them too late and you may never get the chance to influence their purchase decision.

Today's buyers are mentally "almost there" when they walk in. They are predisposed to deal today if they are treated right. Personality and disposable income are the key determinants as to how these buyers reach their purchase decisions. They may have been researching the internet for weeks, understand all the product details and competitive pricing – or they may know very little and need to be guided through their options. Their purchase criteria might even be pretty loose – "I want to buy a new shirt and I will know it when I see it."

> THEY DON'T WEAR a special hat proclaiming, "I am a buyer."

In stores that have Qmatic's "check-in" process, the buyer could access the right type of help when they are ready to receive it. But let's assume that we are in a retail store where such a system is still a future possibility.

First the sales person has to correctly identify that the customer he is observing is one of the important "Today's Buyers." If the sales person approached customers at random until he got a "hit," this would be a very wasteful process. The alternatives are to either hang back and wait for a customer to approach you, or try to understand the customer's need through observation.

> IT IS IMPOSSIBLE to distinguish between the three types with the naked eye.

It's a difficult call to identify a serious buyer from visual cues. Sales people need patience and an open mind, and must be ready for anything.

Having identified that a customer wants assistance, what kind of help does he need? What level of knowledge is required to address the customer's question? Where will the conversation start – with a query about stock availability of this particular model, or a treatise on the flat-screen TV market?

Researchers

The second category consists of the "Researchers." These people are gathering information for a future purchase and are unlikely to deal on this visit. That said, a timely intervention by a knowledgeable sales person could influence their research process by adding a vital snippet of information about the product or service proposition from this store which they would not have otherwise picked up. If this new information is sufficiently dramatic it may even shift them from "Researcher" to "Today's Buyer."

Researchers are prospective buyers. They will make a purchase but not necessarily from your store and probably not today. But it's vital to get key information to researchers in order to influence the outcome of their decision making process. What better time to do that than in the environment that you control – your store. If you wait until they go home and look up the information on the internet, your ability to orchestrate the answers they find has diminished.

Researchers will look and behave exactly like Today's Buyers but they will prove difficult to engage with and almost impossible to close a sale with – unless they hear something new that shakes their views about the product.

Earlier in this book I highlighted the electricals retailer that had a deliberate policy of preventing staff from assisting customers with low-value purchases. In fact, low-value purchases are a useful path for Researchers to experience a brand and feel their way towards a larger, more expensive purchase. A timely

> **LOW-VALUE PURCHASES let Researchers experience a brand and feel their way towards more expensive purchases.**

intervention by knowledgeable staff can not only secure a small purchase today, it can provide a step on the path to a bigger purchase tomorrow.

Focussing on the lifetime value of a customer relationship transforms business models. A first sale might be accomplished through clever advertising, pricing or brand ambience but subsequent success will depend upon the brand's ability to deliver on its promise. Excellent customer service can help brands leap to "trusted advisor" status in a shopper's mind, forming a strong affinity that produces revenue and satisfaction. In my experience this approach leads to loyal customers, consistent sales delivery and long-term margin development.

Just looking – really, just looking

The final category really are "Just Looking." These people are sheltering from the rain or accompanying someone from one of the first two categories. Their chief purpose in life appears to be to provide your valuable sales people with false targets to waste their time on. But they might be influencers who will be asked questions by a Researcher after they leave the store together, "What did you think of their price promise?" Or they may comment about the way the salesman approached

> THEIR CHIEF PURPOSE in life is to provide your valuable sales people with false targets to waste their time on.

them, "I didn't like his supercilious attitude – just because we didn't buy something today." So they may not be Today's Buyers but they could be Today's Naysayers if you don't treat them nicely.

WHEN I FIRST STARTED BROADCASTING I was given some great advice by a then editor of BBC's Panorama, who administered my gruelling media training: "Treat every question as if it was loaded and every microphone as if it was live."

Likewise, I would say to anyone tasked with selling in retail space, treat every visitor you see and every conversation you have as if it's the only sale you are going to make. The more conversations you have the more you will sell, and who knows, that shambling, scruffy individual might be an undercover shopper who will report back to head office on you.

11
PLANET RETAIL

I'm a demanding shopper. Treat me right and I may just buy something. I want what I want. And I want it now. And that means I want service when I need it too.

MEET THE 21ST-CENTURY SHOPPER. It's you. It's me. It's all of us. We have so much choice. There are now more stores than ever, offering a vast array of things for us to buy.

Retail stores are about experience and instant gratification – as many as 75% of purchase decisions are made in store. Coupled with the findings that up to 60% of a business's customers are ready to defect to another store – of whom 43% do so because of service issues – it becomes obvious that in today's retail world, service makes all the difference.[7]

The best retailers know this. A strong service offer can shift the basis for the comparison of offers between competing brands. Done well it can help consumers appreciate the difference between "value" and "cheap." If a product offer is more expensive because it has features that better fit my needs or aspirations, then I will be prepared to pay a premium price for it. However, take away the service offer that explains the difference between this one and the cheapest, and the argument is lost to a straight comparison of price. Of course, a strong price proposition can sit comfortably alongside a strong service offer, for instance John Lewis's "Never knowingly undersold" philosophy, which simply states that you won't be overcharged for what you buy from the store, and they commit to providing you with the best service that they can offer.

The fact is that people like people. Timely and effective service intervention at key moments in the shopper's journey through the store can make all the difference to the experience.

In the earlier chapters we looked at how lean service delivery can liberate resources. Let's now examine in more detail the other important aspect of face-to-face delivery – cash-taking.

PAY HERE

The placement of cash registers remains a contentious issue for some brands. Store designers seem to see these things as a necessary evil, taking up space that could otherwise be occupied by more merchandise. But the registers are an integral stage in the customer's journey. At the end of their shopping trip through the store, customers want to be able to see where the registers are and know that a member of staff is available to serve them.

Too many retailers still get it quite wrong. It starts with customers not being able to locate a cash register or finding no staff present to serve them. And then because the store planners have not recognised that customers will have to wait, there is no management of the resultant queue for service. A line forms back through the aisles of merchandise because there is nowhere else to stand and this blocks access for other customers who are still shopping. Customers arrive at the registers from more than one direction and so it's not obvious who should get served next – raising the stress levels of customers and staff alike. As staff come under pressure, transactions become rushed, and questions about the store experience aren't asked. As customers come under pressure, they overlook the products on the impulse-buy shelf, reducing potential basket size.

It's not hard to get it right. If the tills are scattered around the shop floor they are harder to spot from where the customer is standing; much better if they are all together in a big block with a sign overhead saying "Pay Here." The best location for this big block is on the customer's natural journey through the store – chances are they will leave the store the way they came in. If they walked past the bank of tills on their way in or while ascending the stairs, then they should be able to find it on the way out too.

> STORE DESIGNERS see cash registers as a necessary evil, taking up space that could be occupied by more merchandise.

Moreover, if all the registers are in a single bank, it's also easier to have the right number of staff dedicated to cash-taking. Staffing becomes much more scalable between peak and off-peak periods, and with just one queue to monitor it's obvious to staff and their management when another register needs to be opened.

When we add a Call Forward System to this – and assuming there are four or more registers – the efficiency savings are further increased. Stores can then choose between (a) investing the same number of counter hours to cash-taking as before, thus eliminating the waiting lines of customers much more easily, and (b) reducing counter hours, and hence keeping wait times the same as before but returning staff to the shop floor to assist customers with their shopping.

A recent study, carried out by Qmatic in the UK, suggests that for a number of retailers with large-format stores and scattered cash registers, as many of one-fifth of the tills and one-fifth of staff hours could be removed with no detrimental effect on waiting times. If the full efficiency gain was monetised, this would be worth up to £100 million a year in savings for a large chain.

The survey also showed that 93% of shoppers preferred cash registers to have Call Forward – proof of the wide recognition that the system has won for helping to speed things up.

Having registers standing idle in store is bad for shopper morale. If customers are waiting to get served it's better to see only five registers fully staffed and in use than to have another two or three that are never used. The sight of unoccupied registers at busy times drives a customer's perception that the store is not committed to delivering great service. Removing the registers that are never staffed will remove a negative impression for the waiting customer.

> **HAVING REGISTERS standing idle in store is bad for shopper morale.**

A bank of registers, correctly laid out, with a linear queue in front of it, and incorporating impulse merchandising, can become a business unit in its own right – its operational costs can be measured, and its sales potential from the items displayed in the line can be very significant. Provided that the right range of impulse merchandise is selected and correctly displayed, additional sales can reach up to £1,200 per week per linear metre of displayed product. With two metres per queue and across a 500-store chain, that would add £25 million of additional revenue per year.

DO-IT-YOURSELF CHECKOUTS

Not everything that retailers do in store delivers better, faster service. An increasing number of stores in the UK and the USA are rolling out self-scan checkouts, where customers scan their own items, bag up their goods, pay and leave, in theory without having to talk to any member of the staff.

There seem to be two key drivers for these devices' popularity among retailers. The first is that by allowing the customer to undertake check-out for themselves, the stores can reduce staff hours committed to cash-taking. The second belief is that because customers are significantly more occupied by coping with the full transaction unaided, they perceive the transaction to be taking less time – when in fact it takes more.

In stores where there are both staffed and self-scan registers available to customers, the typical basket size processed through self-scan is slightly smaller and the transactions generally take around 20% longer. Manufacturers of self-scan technology habitually claim that this is

> THEY PERCEIVE the transaction to be taking less time – when in fact it takes more.

because customers are currently unfamiliar with the technology and will get quicker with use. However, I believe that this argument is not the complete story. There are several reasons why self-scan checkouts are inherently slower than staffed checkouts:

1. Staff who operate checkouts do so on a very regular basis and become very familiar with their operation, much more so than any consumer will become through a weekly shop. There is no reason to believe

that a customer will ever reach the same speed of operation working by himself.

2. In some situations a member of staff still needs to be present, to ascertain a shopper's age, for instance, if they are buying alcohol or solvents. Or if the shopper makes an error, the transaction cannot be completed until a member of staff comes to the rescue. These interruptions slow down the whole transaction, which in turn lengthens queueing time for all those customers waiting to use a self-scan checkout.

Ironically a number of supermarkets are putting self-scan registers in their express lanes – and slowing things down as a result.

Self-scan's real role in life is twofold. Although the technology is at this time more expensive than a standard manned register, the savings it can generate in staff hours produce a return-on-investment argument. It also allows the store to liberate a member of staff and put him into a more proactive role helping shoppers to shop. For customers who prefer to serve themselves – be they embarrassed husbands buying "feminine hygiene" products, or just shoppers who prefer doing rather than waiting (even though it's slower) – self-scan is a godsend.

ONE IN FRONT

In 1999, Tesco introduced a "One in front" policy, where if there was more than one customer queueing in front of you, they would open another checkout. (The inevitable caveat was that this would be done provided there were sufficient staff and checkouts available of course.)

When the strategy was introduced it relied on manual measurement of queue lengths, with cashiers prompted to log the number of people in their queue. By 2008 the chain had invested in heat-seeking cameras that could sense the number of customers entering the store and predict the number of checkouts needed. "We can monitor and manage the service customers get more precisely – by customer, by store and by the minute," said Tesco chief executive, Terry Leahy. "Thanks to this, a quarter of a million more customers every week don't have to queue." When Tesco announced their annual results in 2008, they attributed their increase in sales and market share to putting the needs of customers first with innovations such as "One in front."

CHECKOUT THE LAYOUT

Until now food retailers have been ultra-conservative with the layout of their checkouts. No one, for instance, has yet been brave enough to look seriously at how linear queues could be implemented for shopping carts, although several chains have discussed the idea. Its implementation would likely reduce customers' choice of lanes from more than 20 down to around three, with each of the three linear queues served by around eight belted checkouts. The queue would be "buffered," meaning that the next customer would be called to put their goods on the belt while the first customer was being served – this would keep productivity levels at the checkout as high as they are today.

The key advantage of such a set-up would be that while the mean waiting time would be the same, the variation around it would be markedly reduced, so that no customers would have to wait exceptionally long times. It would also signal an end to that frustrating moment when staff tell you that their lane is closed just as you get there. It may even make the stores more shoppable by moving the queues out of the aisles of merchandise, helping navigation for those customers

> IT WOULD SIGNAL the end to that moment when staff tell you that their lane is closed just as you get there.

who are still shopping. The potential for impulse merchandising would also be increased for all customers in store.

While self-scan registers may represent a new frontier in service allocation, the way that most retailers have installed the technology in store is, to say the least, unfortunate. Typically, staffed registers have been removed and a greater number of self-scan devices plonked down in the same space with little thought given as to how customers wait for access to one of these devices.

The potential for multiple queues and queue jumping significantly increases the tension between customers which is exacerbated when half way through their transaction they are forced to wait for a member of staff to arrive in order to move the shopping process along.

If self-scan is to become a permanent part of our shopping experience then the micro-layout of this part of the store needs to be considered carefully and sufficient staff made available to support it adequately and to ensure customers are not left to fend for themselves while the waiting queue quietly seethes. There is a definite potential for a Call Forward solution which if executed correctly would help to speed the flow and increase the efficiency of these devices.

MAPPING THE CUSTOMER'S JOURNEY

There is no mystery about great service. It's a repeatable process that can be consistently delivered by well-trained, highly motivated staff who are supported by appropriate systems. You just need all of those things to make it work!

Best practice in service delivery involves mapping customers' possible journeys through the store, and thinking through the interactions that they will need to have – either with staff or some form of self-service device – in order to complete their shopping mission today.

Once this map has been created, the retailer needs to then consider how the staff interactions will be managed, not just in their flagship stores but across the entire store network. A store brand must not only have a consistent look and feel across its network, it must deliver a consistent service experience if it is going to make its physical premises pull their weight in the age of internet shopping. Just how will the service be near closing time in that small store in a provincial town? Will the service in a busy city-centre store at lunchtime be any better? Will front-line staff still be eager to deliver great service if they feel under pressure through excessive paperwork?

> **A STORE BRAND must deliver a consistent look and service experience across all its branches.**

Technology can help. Solutions like Qmatic's Matchmaker can register how many customers request service, ensure that qualified service is delivered to them within an acceptable wait time, and even record whether or not a sale was made, and, if not, why not. Such systems offer more than queue management; they also offer an "audit" of the sales process, supporting the measurement of demand and the effectiveness of the sales team in delivering against it. They can thus lead to improvement in the quality of service delivered, in the cost per transaction of service delivery, and the provision of strategically important factual feedback about the sales process to key decision makers across the business in a timely way.

What's more, such technology opens a gateway to finding efficiencies in service delivery across an entire network of stores. For example, on checking-in for service at one branch, a customer might find that the waiting time for an expert at that branch may be unacceptable, but the advice they need could be available immediately from someone in another branch. A simple video link would provide the human interaction that they need to achieve a purchase.

It's great service like this that will deliver more loyal customers who will increase their basket size on this visit and come back for more. On Planet Retail, where the customer can easily walk out and give his business to any one of your many competitors, this is the only way to fly.

12

THE
RETAIL SAFARI

Try as you might it's hard to be completely dispassionate about your own business. We all think that we are pretty good, that we work hard and that we are doing a great job. It's easy to get so wrapped up in the detail of running the business that you stop seeing it the way that your customers do. You forget that they lack your familiarity with it and your confidence in communicating with it. It's a short leap from here to arrogance and complacency – and that kills businesses.

ROCKING THE BOAT

Back to Peugeot again where, with one particular dealer, I used to get frustrated arguing with him about his customer facilities. Dealers are franchisees, meaning that he owned his own business and made his own decisions about how he ran it. I could influence him, I could cajole and threaten him, but I couldn't make him do anything he didn't want to do. Working in that style of relationship with all of my dealers and wanting to succeed in my career, I quickly learned the power of persuasion.

I found that when change is initiated from within, when a business really wants to do it, it's a powerful thing.

In this case we had been skirmishing for months around his "customer experience" – what it was like to be a customer of his business. I just couldn't get him to see my point. Simple things like having clearly labelled customer parking, the state of decoration of the showroom, the way his staff answered the telephone – he just didn't see the need to spend the money and the time on changing things.

In a moment of inspiration I offered to take him out for a day to look at the subject of customer experience. To shut me up, he agreed. We fixed on a date two weeks hence to give me time to prepare. That morning, I picked him up at 8 a.m. and we headed for a town about 50 miles away. He was still in the dark as to my precise intentions.

WHEN CHANGE IS INITIATED from within, when a business really wants to do it, it's a powerful thing.

Our business, cars, was typically the second most expensive purchase that most people make. I needed to get my man out of his comfort zone and get him thinking like a customer of service rather than a supplier. We were going to go house shopping for the day.

Initially he was very sceptical, but I got him to bear with me through the experience. I was young, intense and most likely being a pain. First of all, over coffee in a local hotel we talked about the kind of house he currently lived in and what he liked and disliked about it. Then we went on to think about why he might want to move. Armed with this scenario we went off to meet some estate agents. I had arranged the day so that in total we would mystery shop twelve agents, six in person and six on the phone. He would do the talking, I the observing, and then we would compare notes after each call.

We walked through the door of the first office. There was paper piled everywhere, dirty coffee cups on the desks, telephones ringing unanswered in the background. In a corner of the office three untroubled sales people were talking to one other in a leisurely fashion. Our arrival was cordially ignored for seven minutes that felt like a lifetime. My dealer became impatient. "Come on," he said, "I'm not standing for this." And then we were gone.

When we were back in the car I asked him how he felt about his experience. At first he found it difficult to articulate his feelings but as the day wore on he gradually found his words.

He told me that in the first office he felt angry at being ignored and stressed by the surroundings he found himself in. Seven minutes of waiting in this situation had been enough to push him away from using that business at any foreseeable time in the future.

I had arranged things so that the first few contacts he experienced were as dire as I could make them and then gradually I exposed him to better, more professional, treatment. He got the message.

By late afternoon he understood the psychology of the situation. Unlike in the car showroom, where he felt very comfortable, as a house hunter in an agent's office he was in someone else's territory and just the act of walking in was stress-inducing.

PAPER piled everywhere, dirty coffee cups on the desks...

In the better offices they had developed and honed the skill for allowing customers to "land" in the office at their own pace before greeting each customer and offering help and advice at just the right moment – too early would elicit the defensive brush off, "I'm just looking thank you," too late and the moment was gone. Putting the customer at ease, and providing supportive, empathetic service, ensured the customer was in the right frame of mind to do business, and that the brand value of "trusted advisor" was communicated through the actions of the staff.

Now it was time to repeat the exercise but bring it closer to home. I took him to the most successful car dealership in town. He looked at the rows of gleaming secondhand cars; we parked without difficulty in clearly designated customer parking. We walked into the brightly painted showroom where we were greeted warmly by the receptionist who asked how he could help us and offered us coffee.

In the car, on the way back to his place, he was remarkably quiet. I could almost hear his brain working.

His experience of the estate agents had made him realise how it felt to be a hesitant, unconfident customer walking into his showroom. He now understood the impact of each event on the customer's journey – from the way the staff handled the customer's initial phone call through the ambience of the place and on to the attitude of the staff when they dealt with the customer face to face. He now understood the importance of appearing knowledgeable but behaving without arrogance, building the confidence of the customer to do a deal through trust. In future he used this approach in training all the staff who joined him.

I looked forward to my next trip to see him and a month later when I pulled up on his forecourt I was not disappointed. Staff cars had been banished to the rear of the premises and fresh white lines painted on the swept tarmac to indicate customer parking. There was even a sign. Climbing out of my car I took a good hard look at the showroom. What was different?

That's it – you could see in. Ten years' worth of old posters and grime had been painstakingly removed and the glass positively sparkled. They had even washed the Peugeot signs. As I walked through the showroom door the difference hit me immediately. It was warm! Not only had the interior been repainted in pastel colours and the carpet cleaned but someone had turned the heat on and put a pot of coffee on to brew. There were carefully planned displays of accessories and brochures. None of the changes in themselves were expensive or revolutionary, but the cumulative effect was transformational. I could see on the faces of the staff how much happier they were in working there. There was a buzz about the place that made it a pleasant place to be.

The owner greeted me with a big smile and we went into his office. He was so excited that he spent the next half an hour telling me the impact of the changes that he had made. Business was up over 25% and all it had cost was a few hundred pounds in materials and some extra staff hours to make the changes and to hold some meetings about the changes. He was a convert.

START BY THINKING LIKE A SHOPPER

In the queueing business this experiment was translated into the Retail Safari.

The Retail Safari is a great way of getting retailers and bankers back into the mindset of what it feels like to be a customer. They spend so much time looking at the details of their own operations that they forget what it's like to walk through the door as a customer. And even when I ask them to "think like a shopper," retailers invariably backslide into their specialisms. Thus the guys from marketing will look at the display materials – have the stores got the latest posters in the frames? The merchandising manager will look at the new shelves and mentally appraise how well they are standing up to the rigours of shop life.

No one watches their customers.

Over the years I have found myself migrating into the role of customer advocate. When I am researching a prospective customer, and before I approach them, I start by shopping their website, their catalogue – if they have one – and their stores, to find out what it feels like to be a customer. I then think about how that experience could be improved by what I know.

Shopping malls make excellent locations for Retail Safaris. You can compare the offer and delivery of different brands, and there are always a couple of coffee shops – where I like to meet and start off the day.

The first thing I ask them is what they want to get out of our experience together, a question that usually wrinkles foreheads – the look on their faces says, "I thought you were going to tell me?" I ask them to think about the coffee shop we are in. What, ideally do

> SHOPPING MALLS make excellent locations for Retail Safaris.

they want from a coffee shop? "Great coffee" goes without saying but what else? Somewhere to sit. For how long? Say 20 minutes – long enough and comfortable enough to take a break from shopping and chat. Good point – so we need the right ambient noise level, don't we? Not so quiet that it makes people want to whisper but not so loud that they can't talk to each other comfortably. Tables not too close together, for a little privacy and discretion. It should be a relaxed environment, in terms of seating, decor, colour scheme, lighting levels. As these points start growing, we start to build a picture of how to make the shopping experience a superior one.

And what about the staff's role in our coffee shop? Almost every coffee shop has a fundamental problem at the heart of its service process.

> **ALMOST EVERY COFFEE SHOP has a fundamental problem at the heart of its service process.**

As we line up to select our coffee, we make our coffee selection from the big board on the back wall. We order, and they take our money before they make our coffee, to "lock us in." But the problem is, the process of making coffee takes roughly twice as long as taking our cash. A successful coffee store needs to have a production process that can churn out our custom coffee orders at the same pace as it takes cash. The alternative is the chaos that we are all familiar with. It sounds easy when you say it fast. I make my coffee choice, I pay, the cashier writes my name on the side of the cup, the cup is passed along to the barista who fills it with hot, frothy coffee. But the cashier has misheard my name and spelt it incorrectly. The barista may apply his own logic to which drink he makes first in the interests of getting through the backlog faster. The cramped conditions behind the service counter don't help in keeping the process orderly, and to add to the chaos some customers need their paninis heated. When I join the other customers waiting at the end of the counter I am quickly confused as to which coffee belongs to whom – not helped by a barista who mumbles as he slaps them on the counter and moves on to the next one. The process

154

is chaotic and confusing – not the relaxed, laid-back feeling that exists throughout the rest of the store.

These things quickly and easily undermine the great brand strategy that was set at head office because the operational detail hasn't been thought through – no one has played customer advocate and considered how that moment of truth, when we pay and get our coffee, actually feels.

That's why the coffee shop is a great place to start the Retail Safari – it's a neutral space which allows my group to get into a "shopper's mindset" and consider all retail space from a customer's point of view. Having established this we can then get on to the heart of the safari.

HITTING THE STREETS

At our first safari stop, we pause outside the store to consider the external appearance. Signs, branding and window displays influence the way prospective customers feel about the brand and its current relevance to them, attracting the attention of those who may not have planned to visit the store today but whose imagination is captured by something there.

The dilemma with many retail locations is, to what extent do you allow the customer to see through the window and into the store? It's important to take a passing customer on a journey of discovery that makes them want to enter the store. The brand signage, merchandise and offers in the window and the view of the store can accomplish this when the customer is a target customer for the store and the job is done well. Large posters that completely obscure the window can bring this process to a halt – unless they have a compelling message on them like "Sale! One day only! 70% off!" Some stores deliberately create exclusivity around their brand by obscuring the windows. There is a balance to be struck here between making a brand aspirational and having no customers to serve.

Next, is the store entrance clear and inviting? What if I am pushing a pram or I'm in a wheelchair? The store needs to be as inclusive as possible, maximising the number of people who can successfully use it and enjoy the experience.

How well is the "landing strip" managed? Shoppers use the first two metres or so to slow down and adjust to the store environment – getting their bearings, deciding where they need to go. A common mistake is to put things that you want the customer to see too close to the store entrance and so as the customer enters the store he is already past them before he realises that they are there. If that was a stack of baskets back there the customer is now limited in how much he can select and carry. If it was wayfinding signage then it's now much more challenging for the customer to find his way around the store.

> **SHOPPERS USE the first two metres to slow down and adjust to the store environment.**

A shopper's attention is like a searchlight with a variable beam. If the shopper is relaxed, the beam's focus is wide – he looks around, drinking in the surroundings, happy to be entertained and amused. But if he is stressed, the searchlight becomes tightly focussed – he prowls back and forth, looking for the one thing that he wants to find, and then it's really hard to attract his attention for anything else.

So we have made it inside the store and we are moving to the department we want to be in. We touch the merchandise, we pick it up and examine it; we might decide to buy and or we might keep browsing. Maybe we need help. Imagine we are planning to buy an expensive TV and trying to understand the differences between the available products. How does the store handle the situation? What do we as consumers want to happen at this point? The first thing we want is control. We want polite, relevant and insightful advice based on reassuring expertise. This gives us the confidence that we are going to be guided to the right choice for our requirements (not stitched up with the most expensive thing on sale or treated with contempt by someone who couldn't care less and knows less than we do). It's not much to ask is it? After all, the store has gone to all of the trouble of stocking and displaying these goods. Is it really so unreasonable to expect the staff to be able to tell us something about them? And if it is – why bother having any staff at all? Why not just have rows of product that we can look at and when we want to ask a question or buy the product make us go onto the internet?

If we are planning to make a purchase now and we are in your store considering which product to buy, and with a little effort you can close the sale, why not do it – when the alternative is that we keep shopping in your competitors' stores and on the internet until we sell ourselves something or a great sales person in a competing store delivers the help, advice and service we are looking for?

So now the first part of our journey is complete. We came, we saw, we selected and now, carrying our purchase with us, it's time to pay and get out of there.

But hang on, where do I pay? I am looking around the shop floor and I can see four or five locations where there are registers – but it's a Tuesday afternoon and the store is quiet – which register is staffed? I should have brought my binoculars – this is ridiculous. Ok – I have it figured out – it's the one over in the corner and I can see some people waiting to pay, so over I go. I stand where I think I should to show that I am next behind the lady in the fawn coat but then someone else arrives

IT'S THE WRAP-UP, the moment of truth, the chance to ask the customer how everything was today.

and stands next to us. The cashier finishes what she is doing (what was she doing – isn't she supposed to be serving?) and looks at the guy in the glasses who is standing next to us and she serves him! She serves him? How do I feel? Outraged – that's how I feel.

Making that last experience of the store perfect can overcome any shortfalls that the shopper experiences throughout the journey; making a mess of it can ruin all the good work done before. It's the wrap-up, the moment of truth, a chance to ask the customer how everything was today. It's an empowering situation that allows the shopper to "get it off their chest," and if the feedback process is handled correctly, even a bad experience can become a great one.

So this is the experience I expose retailers and bankers to. The opportunity to feel what it's like to be a customer in their stores. By contrasting the in-store experience between different stores in a shopping centre or in a town, I make them better, more discerning shoppers who are able to understand the customer's point of view. It's a defining moment which demonstrates graphically the issues which remain abstract when discussed over a desk in head office. It brings the customer's viewpoint to life.

13

LOVE ME, LOVE MY BRANCH

RETAILERS AND BANKS OCCUPY similar spaces in our High Streets and shopping malls, and in recent years banks have aspired to become more like retailers in the way they interact with customers. But the banks are different – whether they like it or not.

The banking industry had been slow to catch on to the benefits of queue management, but with the help of our guerrilla sales force – the general public – we had persuaded them that they should manage the waiting experience in their branches better. Pretty soon the familiar cry of "Cashier Number Three Please!" was being heard throughout busy city-centre branches all over the UK.

If the banks showed any reluctance in engaging with us then it flowed from their ambivalence towards the role of the branch in their channel strategy: Did they really want customers to visit their branches at all?

A senior executive of a Scottish bank described this to me over dinner one night.

"You see," he explained, "When telephone banking was introduced there was a common belief that branches would disappear from the high street – we just wouldn't need them anymore. A proportion of customers took to telephone banking for the everyday transactional stuff – checking balances, transferring funds, paying bills. And the widespread deployment of automated teller machines (ATMs) further drove traffic away from inside the branches. If customers need cash they don't even have to cross our doorstep."

With the advent of internet banking, that should have been the ultimate nail in the coffin for branch banking. If we could carry out our research, get our questions answered, and conduct all of our transactions electronically, then why did we still need branches?

When the industry created each new service – first telephone banking and then internet banking – they were trying to drive down the cost of transacting business with customers. Processing all of those cheques and individual actions within each branch was prohibitively expensive. By automating these low-value transactions and centralising resources they could achieve massive efficiencies of scale.

THE ROLE OF THE BRANCH PERSISTS

The banks expected telephone and internet banking to reduce the demand for branches. But it didn't work quite the way they intended.

Most customers used a mixture of all three channels: the internet for basic transactions and research; the telephone for queries which couldn't be answered by the standard FAQs on the website; and the branch for serious money work, thinking about mortgage applications or savings products.

This put the industry in a serious dilemma. The branches had not been eliminated because they were still seen by customers as a necessary way of transacting more complex business. But the new channels had eaten away at the "showroom traffic levels" – the number of customers and prospects that would walk into the branch and provide someone to sell to, a sales channel that would help make sense of the cost of branch infrastructure.

The only way forward was to make the branches work harder as "brand showrooms" creating opportunities for the banks to sell to us, their customers and their prospects.

AN ICON OF TRUST

Branches came back into fashion. They represented a unique environment, usually co-located with the places where we shop, in which the bank could manage our journey through their offer and attempt to surprise and delight us.

When it comes to buying a pension, taking out a major loan or a mortgage, the majority of customers still prefer to sit across a desk from an expert and complete the process face to face. This process was uniquely suited to the branch environment.

Branch closure programmes slowed. They didn't halt altogether – it was still necessary, particularly as the banking industry continued to consolidate, to ensure that each branch was positioned in an area with sufficient customer potential to support it – but now the emphasis changed, to recognise the role that branches could play in promoting the banking industry as enablers of consumers' dreams.

Even after all of the consolidation programmes so far, there are still some 500,000 bank branches around the world. In the medium term, at least, that number will be maintained and may even grow as banks compete to introduce their services to the newer economies while maintaining their iconic presence in the main streets of more mature economies.

Over the last ten years the pendulum has swung in favour of the branch. The industry embraced the new paradigm with enthusiasm, many hiring senior staff from retailers in order to embed the philosophy required to think and act in the desired way.

Along came the design houses to help the banks showcase their brand values in their high-street premises. The banks had always done this, but previously the values they communicated had been dictated by the priorities of a previous era. In Victorian times the banking industry built huge Gothic premises resembling religious buildings which served to pronounce their role in society as pillars of the community, whose longevity was underpinned by the awesome majesty of the buildings that they created. These monstrosities were used to set in stone the style of relationship the bank wanted to have with their customers: serious-minded, authoritarian, permanent.

> THE ONLY WAY forward was to make the branches work harder as "brand showrooms."

A new generation of designers was hired to reflect the position the industry wanted to attain in its consumers' minds. The balance of power had shifted towards consumer choice. Banks wanted to appear friendly, caring and innovative – facilitators of positive change in consumers' lives.

Substantial sums were committed to branch refurbishment projects, with some experimentation taking place in the process. In the UK, for instance, Abbey National tried out a joint venture that saw coffee shops being put inside their premises; however, although this experiment created a rental income from dead space inside some of the larger branches, the new owners, Santander, did not pursue it.

Across the industry, there was a massive move towards the use of display technology inside branches and within window presentations. The use of digital media has become part of everyone's lives and if the banks could successfully embrace it then this would help to shape the environment of the branch. Sadly, such efforts have been largely unsuccessful, sometimes because of lack of vision in seeing a strategy through, other times because displays have been placed in branch with little thought as to how customers or staff would use them. In their eagerness to communicate, the banks lost the thread of what they were ultimately trying to achieve – a usable environment where customers could quietly assimilate new information about the bank's offer and where they could access help and advice when they needed it.

> IN TRYING TO introduce a "glamour factor," the banks ignored some of the basic housekeeping.

The huge sums that banks spent on refurbishing branches often did not result in a clear payback, reported the *McKinsey Quarterly Journal* in 2007. "The problem arose when banks adopted an intuitive design approach that emphasises aesthetics and expensive format changes, overlooking customers' needs. Instead banks should put utility before appearances, favour low budget tactical adjustments and use branch formats to manage customer visits actively."[8]

This was a damning indictment of the banking industry's early approach to innovation in the branch environment and showed that there was a need to embrace change differently. In trying to introduce a "glamour factor" into the branches, the banks had ignored some of the basic housekeeping.

I undertook a number of studies at this time to look at the way customers used branches, and the issues and frustrations that this led to.

ACCESSING SERVICE IN THE BRANCH

There are essentially three types of activity that customers want to undertake in a bank branch. Each requires a different level of knowledge and training to serve:

- At the simplest level, customers have a straightforward transaction – withdrawing cash, making a payment, checking a balance – and this can be accomplished in many cases on an ATM without reference to a member of staff. A percentage of customers prefer to use counter service for such transactions; many have been successfully migrated to using the technology unaided.

- At the next level of complexity, we might have a query, or a change to make to our account, requiring us to interact with a member of staff.

- At the highest level, we might need guidance and expert input into the choice of a complex financial product.

Traditionally, banks in the UK and the US have operated a linear queue in branch which feeds a line of teller positions, so that relatively short and transactional needs can be served at the counter. Increased use of ATMs in the branch has led to the reduction in the number of teller positions.

Tellers now, however, also play a vital interactive role in selling the bank's products and services to their customers. This initiative – to turn "tellers into sellers" – has played a major role in branch reconfiguration, with many banks introducing software at the tellers' terminals that prompts them to ask a relevant question of the customer standing in front of them during the course of the transaction. This could be as simple as, "Mr Customer, I notice that you have a large balance on your current account. Do you have a special purpose in mind for this money or would you like to consider moving the balance to a savings account where you could earn some interest on it?" This approach has led to an uplift in business for the banks and helped customers to understand how the bank's offer can help them more.

> **TELLERS INTO SELLERS:**
> Tellers now sell the bank's products and services to their customers.

One of the biggest problems, though, is the way this lengthens each transaction at the counter. At busy times this has a knock-on effect on queueing times – increasing customer frustration.

The issue at the nub of this is that the stressed teller, who can see the queue building up, asks his question and receives a positive response from the customer in front of him and now has to find a means to get that customer served by another member of the bank staff so that he can return to serving the waiting line of customers. Until this handover is made, the teller is blocked by the customer standing in front of him.

Access to staff for the more complex discussions in branch can also be problematic. Normally banks have used a reception desk, a help and advice counter or a member of staff front of house who "meets and greets." In theory any of these approaches sounds fine; the difficulty comes as the branch becomes more loaded with customers who want service. A customer arriving in a busy lunchtime slot is likely to be confronted by queues of waiting customers at every turn. A line for the tellers, a line for the ATMs, and a line for the reception desk. In such circumstances, even for customers who have a pre-booked appointment, the process of checking-in can be a tense and frustrating experience.

MAKING AN APPOINTMENT

Banks have used appointment systems to reschedule demand for their staff resource in branch. It's quite common for expensive resource, for example a mortgage specialist, to be shared among several branches – he will be in a particular branch on a given day and have appointments made for him in that branch on that day. A customer arriving on a different day will be out of luck and will need to schedule a future appointment when the mortgage person is in residence.

However, appointment systems are not quite the panacea that banks would like to believe. Despite the banks' acknowledging the appointment when it is made and reminding the customer the day before it arrives, the incidence of customers not turning up at all or turning up either very late or early is very high – often exceeding 30%.

It's not just banking that suffers from this problem. We consumers have to accept our share of the blame for this. In the UK, the National Health Service loses thousands of hours of valuable clinic time from patient "no-shows." In August 2005 the Sunday Telegraph reported that missed appointments cost the NHS £575 million a year.[9] Around 11.3% of all outpatient appointments in England were no-shows, with a further 10% cancelled by patients in advance, and around 12% cancelled by hospitals.

> THE INCIDENCE of customers turning up very late or very early or not at all is very high – often exceeding 30%.

The report highlighted a number of initiatives in progress to try to reduce this. Four years later, the same newspaper reported that there were 6.5 million skipped appointments in Britain between 2007 and 2008, with hospitals losing around £100 every time a patient did not show up.[10] Despite the best efforts of the NHS to improve matters it would appear that the problem is getting worse, with the cost for missed appointments rising to nearer £650 million a year. If the health service cannot compel patients to attend clinics for health-related issues what chance do the banks have of persuading customers to comply with their pre-booked appointments?

When a customer books a slot with a service provider they block that slot out of the provider's capacity model, preventing any other customer from accessing it. If a percentage of customers don't turn up, the service provider's productivity level must suffer to the same extent. In the case of the NHS if almost all patients are seen in clinics through pre-booked appointments and the "no-show" rate is 11% then 11% of capacity is wasted, at huge, non-productive cost to the UK taxpayer. It also means that patients waiting for a future appointment must wait 11% longer than they would otherwise have to.

The banking industry's purpose in using appointment-setting systems is twofold: To offer a better service to customers through the promise of a qualified resource in an agreed future time slot, and to attempt to match available serving capacity to demand levels and raise productivity, ensuring a competitive cost structure.

However, this plan has unintended consequences. Let's say that a bank schedules 70% of its mortgage experts' hours for appointment customers, and "sells" these appointments to customers who telephone or request service via the internet. Let's assume that the "no-show" rate is 20%. If 20% of pre-booked appointment customers don't turn up, then 14% of the bank's entire mortgage experts' time will be wasted. That's a massive additional overhead to carry within the business. Conversely customers who walk in off the street – provided that their check-in process is handled correctly and they can be seen by an expert, perhaps after a short wait – are unlikely to disappear, meaning staff hours reserved for walk-ins can be much more productive. Well, if only we could predict how many customers will come in and when they will arrive!

If a mortgage expert, or any other specialist resource, is booked for an appointment in branch, but that customer has not yet arrived, at what stage does the bank free up the resource to see another waiting customer?

Real-life choices are faced by staff every day as they try to deliver the best service that they can, with the available resource that they have, to whoever turns up to experience it. I have been able to witness this story from both sides. I have seen customers arrive at a branch to see an expert and be asked to wait for an undefined and often unforgivably long period of time and accept it as the norm. I have also sat with branch managers who, at the end of a busy day, and armed with the complex scientific outputs from the bank's IT system, have manually rewritten onto a sticky note the Name, Appointment Time and Purpose for each pre-booked customer appointment for the next day, and affixed each one of these sticky notes to a wall chart. By this means they sought to get an overview of what resource they had available and when. Pre-booked appointments are generally allocated a large percentage of the bank's sales capacity and so any variation in the time customers arrive or if they don't arrive at all can have a devastating effect on the manager's plan for the day. While the whiteboard approach can provide a snapshot before the action starts, once the day has got going and customers have started arriving, it's a difficult set of balls to juggle. It's no wonder that staff productivity levels tend to be quite low in such circumstances.

> **WELL IF ONLY we could predict how many customers will come in and when they will arrive!**

WINDS OF CHANGE

It was against this background that a mood shift seemed to come over the banking industry in 2005. Suddenly I found that I was no longer pushing against a completely closed door. The banks were truly ready to embrace queue management as part of their strategy for making branches more effective.

There were many early indications of this through minor projects around branch transformation as organisations wrestled with the task of coping with highly variable demand and finite resource. A number of banks kicked off "Branch of the Future" review projects, examining the way branches operated together with developments in technology which would allow them to do things differently.

But things definitely shifted up a gear for us when in 2005 we were approached by HSBC in the UK to help them think about the customer experience and functionality of their branches. The bank was undertaking a massive £450-million investment programme to create a distinctly different and much more positive customer experience in their branches.

HSBC has over 1700 branches across the UK. In common with all UK banks, it offers counter service for transactions and general enquiries. It also offers many financial products beyond current accounts: mortgages and loans, insurance, savings and credit cards. The start point for the sales process for such products is when the customer walks into a branch in search of advice.

The challenge is that on arrival in the branch, the customer is unsure of where to go, or what to do, to secure the information he needs. This situation is exacerbated if there is a long queue for counter services. The customer may be reluctant to wait just to get information or advice – with the result that he is likely to go elsewhere. Such a scenario has a secondary negative impact for the bank: customers with general enquiries joining the counter queue increase the overall queue length, which can deter other customers from joining it.

Assuming the customer decides to join the queue, he will receive service at the counter. However, counter staff are there to process customers as efficiently as possible, as opposed to selling products, which means that counter staff must call upon back-office colleagues to deal with the product enquiries and sales. This throws up two issues:

- Is there someone immediately available to see the customer?
- Is there someone appropriately qualified to advise the customer and process the sale?

A recognition of these issues, coupled with the fact that HSBC realised the potential impact on the handling of counter customers and potential loss of sales opportunities, drove them to look for a solution.

ENTER THE MATCHMAKER

The Matchmaker software we developed works by having all of the qualifications and areas of expertise of staff logged into a database.

When a customer arrives in the branch, a greeter will ascertain his requirement and use a touch-screen terminal to establish availability of an appropriate adviser. The system checks the availability by qualification and time for sales staff. With this information, the greeter can then either allocate an adviser immediately, or inform the customer of the necessary wait time. If the customer agrees to wait – and they nearly always do – then he is issued with a service receipt that shows the waiting time promise.

Simultaneously the system informs the advisers of the nature of the enquiry, allowing them to prepare and bring appropriate literature and documentation with them.

HSBC initially piloted the Matchmaker system in 20 of its busiest branches, and subsequently implemented it in more than 100 branches. The system went live in 2006 and HSBC estimated that it had already reduced customer waiting times by as much as 20%.

With Matchmaker in place, many aspects of the bank's operations become more efficient. "The system gave managers more control, because they could programme it at the beginning of the day to assign various duties to specific staff members," said Richard Newland of HSBC. "Customers have been impressed with the user-friendly nature of the system, the way our staff interact with them and, of course, the reduction in the time it takes for us to serve them. The system helps

MATCHMAKER works by having all the qualifications and areas of expertise of staff logged into a database.

HSBC stream customers more efficiently, and this reduces the need for unnecessary queueing for counter services with the knock-on effect that it improves the efficiency of that area of the bank's operation as well."

In addition to matching customer needs and staff resource more efficiently, the system has also played a key role in maintaining compliance at all times, by ensuring that only those staff with appropriate qualifications deal with specific types of customer enquiries.

Mr Newland concluded, "Gone are the days when your bank dictated how, where and when you did business with them. You went to a branch between 9.30 a.m. and 3.30 p.m. Monday to Friday and you stood in line, whether you were withdrawing £20 or wanted to apply for a mortgage. Today, customers are looking for more control and greater convenience and efficiency to meet their banking needs, and our branches are designed to do just that."

VIRTUAL QUEUES & SKILLS-BASED ROUTING

HSBC used Qmatic's Matchmaker system to manage the process of check-in and service allocation for walk-in customers needing access to qualified staff. The system maintains a real-time view of the "occupancy" of its qualified sales people and this data, together with the knowledge of their training and skills levels, allows the system to best fit service requests from arriving customers with staff who are available either immediately or soon. Waiting times can thus be estimated before the customers commit to service, effectively resetting their expectations of waiting time. The software keeps a live overview by asking staff to accept or reject offers of arriving customers and by allowing servers to log their current tasks.

Such systems seek to understand the process capability of the serving engine and monitor its performance in real time and then to accept requests for customer service, categorise the customer's request in terms of skill level required and likely duration before committing the service requests to the system, slotting them in where capacity exists. This strategy for resource optimisation in face-to-face service is very effective. Unlike customers who have a pre-booked appointment and who have a high probability of becoming a no-show, walk-in customers are there, physically on the premises. If they can be promised and commit to a time slot for service and that promise can be actively managed to ensure its delivery then the chances of a sale being made are much higher than where no effective service engine exists.

This is innovative thinking within the banking sector in relation to delivering effective, efficient face-to-face service. Queue management systems that allow customers to check in with certain of the banks representatives for a scheduled meeting or to reserve their turn for service in a virtual queue have been supplied successfully for a number of years around the globe. But the Matchmaker software takes things on a considerable stage by applying the discipline of skills-based routing.

Skills-based routing has been used within telephone call centre management for a number of years. By qualifying the needs of a particular customer, that customer can be routed to an expert who has the appropriate expertise to help them. Call centres pioneered the mathematics of achieving this balance of high service levels and optimal efficiency. A.K. Erlang, a mathematician and telephone engineer, examined the issue of how to determine the fewest number of trunk lines necessary to cope

> **THE GREATER YOU CAN POOL resource as opposed to keeping it in isolated buckets, the less of it you need to cope with peak demand.**

with customer demand levels in the early part of the 20th century. One of the principal threads of logic at the heart of his work is that the greater you can pool resource – as opposed to keeping it in isolated buckets – then the less of it you need to cope with peak demand.

To give an example, consider a call-centre scenario in which we have three separate call centres, each with ten operators; calls made to one call centre are handled by one of the ten operators. Erlang found that by modifying the system so that all 30 agents worked as one team, huge gains were to be had: Call-taking capacity would increase; average queue time would decrease; and the number of trunk lines necessary would be significantly reduced.

Banks are increasingly using this principle of synergy across their call centres. Given that a large number of their product experts are sitting in branches waiting for customers, a number of the banks will route "qualified" telephone calls to an expert within the branch to handle that customer's requirement. In the initial part of the call the agent will qualify the customer's need to ensure that they are routed to an expert who has the necessary qualifications and skills to assist the customer; the agent will then forward the call on to an expert.

When one major UK bank did the analysis they found that of the 4 million plus calls that were routed to the branches each year, 42% were lost because either the customer was left hanging on the phone for too long while the expert was being found or the offered call-back took place several days later by which time the customer had taken alternative action. It's a simple-enough sounding problem but it's difficult to fix. Without knowledge of the current occupancy of the experts within the branch, phone calls routed by the primary agents would simply go unanswered until either the customer gave up or they were rerouted back to the call centre.

Using the right problem-solving techniques to attack these issues and implement innovative solutions is already yielding results. One major UK bank has seen a reduction in no-reply/late follow-up to customer calls fall from 20–30% to 4–5% with the help of Cisco Systems' IBSG consultancy arm.

In the future, the integration of Matchmaker software with the bank's IP-based phone system will allow all of the bank's systems to know which qualified experts are currently, or soon to be, available to them across any location within the branch network. Not only will this enable successful call-routing to take place, it will also allow customers who walk into a branch to be connected with an expert in another branch through a video link allowing a "virtual meeting" to take place. While this may not meet the wishes of each and every customer it will provide the vast majority with better, faster service and shorter wait times.

COUNTER QUEUES

Sometimes unacceptable delays in counter queues can be resolved by reorganising the way service is allocated – without requiring extra resource.

I worked with the Halifax Bank of Scotland (HBOS) on a project to apply the "Shortest Process First" methodology to teller queues in branch. We simply took those customers who had just a cheque to pay in and put them into a separate line. Tellers facing this separate, smaller line would serve a customer from the "cheque pay in only" line in priority over the main queue. By this means we processed short transactions first and pulled more customers through the branch faster. The process only works if you have analysed and understood the distribution and frequency of the different transaction types being served at the counter – so there are lots of numbers to crunch before you try it.

This approach was tried out in 12 branches and was a great success. In a number of cases it allowed the branch to hit their "customer service" targets for the first time ever, meaning that queues were managed successfully, customers were happy and staff earned bonuses.

TRANSFORMING THE BRANCH

Branch transformation projects are expensive and resource-hungry. Making effective change stick in a network of a thousand-plus branches requires commitment, consistency and big budgets. The banking sector's record on this subject is not great. There has been a tendency to only cover a small number of branches before a refurbishment project is swept aside by a fresh initiative, leaving the branch network feeling, from a customer's point of view, an inconsistent place in which to do business. I have never understood this partial approach to innovation. If a new idea has defined benefits that survive the decision-making process and get a green light for implementation, why not roll them out and get the full benefits by transforming the entire network? Anything less suggests that the benefits of the change were never clear.

Some initiatives may only be relevant or pay for themselves in certain strata of branches, say the ones that experience the highest customer footfall, but if this is the case, thought needs to be given to how to achieve a consistent look and feel, so that any customer, walking into any branch, enjoys an experience which is consistent with the desired brand values.

In order to innovate in branch successfully, banks need to define their objectives for change and to have a clear understanding of what success looks like. A task-centric innovation approach can provide a consistent framework for this form of change management.

It is necessary to not only understand how customers use the branch today but to consider how they may wish to use it in future. Customer desires and the bank objectives need to be correlated to see how they map together – what changes can the bank make economically which customers will find attractive and useful? Which changes will lead to differentiation and competitive advantage? From this analysis the bank can identify what processes and hardware it needs to update in order to deliver the desired results.

An alternative scenario might be one where vendors compete to offer the banks new technology and new branch formats, which if the vendor's sales effort is successful banks will adopt with no clear idea as to how these changes contribute to an improved business model. In this scenario it is unsurprising that branch transformation projects have often lacked direction and proved unsustainable.

> **UNDERSTAND HOW customers use the branch today, and how they may wish to use it in future.**

Any process of innovation requires discipline in its execution. It also requires open minds, able to consider good ideas wherever they arise. Experimentation is also necessary, testing new concepts before determining if they fit the strategy.

CASE-STUDY: BARCLAYS BANK

Barclays' transformation of their retail branch network began in 2005, with the arrival of Deanna Oppenheimer, now CEO of the retail bank. "We decided that rather than just change the carpet and paint the walls, let's create the next generation of bank branch."

The project pulled together talent and experience from inside the bank and from suppliers, and, crucially, was reinforced by other senior members of the team, Mike Amato and Erin Biertzer, joining from Washington Mutual, where the Occasio project had caused such a stir. Occasio, which in Latin means "favourable opportunity," earned Washington Mutual a patent for its design and much media interest. Using teller pods stationed in the middle of the branch, the "Starbucks-style" open-plan stores with khaki-clad concierges and play areas created a very different environment in which to do banking. Tellers were freed to greet customers as they came through the door and create a more retail feel to the experience.

Mike Amato, now Barclays' global customer transformation director, believes that customer experience needs to drive branch design. "I have seen many instances where banks describe the benefits of branch re-design projects in terms of the financial and efficiency gains to themselves – the customer experience seems to be an afterthought. This is wrong-headed. It's like a CEO saying "Colleagues are our most important resource," and then spending the next two hours talking about the financials."

"It's about creating a great customer experience. If customers feel good about doing business with the bank, they will be more inclined to increase their spending. Better results and efficiencies will flow from there."

The project brief at Barclays was demanding – just 13 weeks from concept to implementation in a live branch in Manchester. During the initial phase, a mock branch was built inside a warehouse in Northampton to test customer and staff reactions to some 30 separate innovations that the team had sourced. "Eight of the new ideas ultimately became part of our branch roll-out programme," says Nic Parmaksizian, now global experience director. "Although each was subject to a return-on-investment test, this was only one of our criteria. We had a series of key performance indicators including impacts on customer satisfaction, colleague satisfaction, waiting time and new business created. We also examined how each idea would impact on the others that we planned to use, seeking to focus on the ones that created the greatest synergies. All of the eight achieved better than our 20% threshold for return on investment."

I was part of the project as a supplier, working alongside nearly fifty others who helped to bring the warehouse stage of the trial together. The degree of cooperation achieved with and between suppliers was impressive. The sheer pace of the project changed the language of the normal customer–supplier relationship, allowing no time for politicking or infighting – just getting on with the job.

The management of the internal team proved to be the harder task. "Great suppliers respond to opportunities because they know that increased business will follow. Managing the internal team and their preconceptions was a different issue," said Mike Amato. He highlighted the difficulty of selling change internally and cited the in-branch counter security glass as an example of the kind of discussions required to move things forward:

"We were clear that we wanted to do away with the glass, but had we just said so, our people would have resisted the change. Security, Risk Management, Human Resources and Operations would all have given reasons why we shouldn't do it. There was a belief that the glass protected our colleagues when in fact all it did was to protect our money. We changed the conversation around by getting our colleagues to think like customers. We asked them a question, 'When you go into the branch as a customer how comfortable are you talking to the teller about your business through the glass?' The team quickly saw this point of view and started to find ways to make it possible to eliminate the glass."

> "WE CHANGED THE conversation around by getting our colleagues to think like customers."

Change was necessary for the bank. "It was clear to everyone that we couldn't begin to think about generating more business until we had dealt with the customer experience issues inside the branch. It was also necessary to properly integrate the Woolwich brand, which we'd bought, into the bank's proposition, and so we had to make sure that we had branches of the right size and in the right locations to deliver the performance we needed." said Mr Amato. In this process the bank moved from around 2,100 branches to 1,700.

To assist in the transformation, Barclays brought in UK retail experience, recruiting Helen Dodd from Tesco where she had spent twenty years working out how to attract retail customers.

The new concept addresses issues of both design and process. Larger areas of glass in the frontage make the branch more welcoming; the use of curves creates a natural, more organic layout; and the use of technology helps to enable – not replace – customer experience. For example, among the many high-tech touches in use at the flagship Piccadilly store is Microsoft's ground-breaking Surface technology. This was the first in bank deployment and it allows users to grab digital content on a screen with their hands and navigate information about products and services with simple gestures and touches. The Surface technology is a 30-inch screen built into a tabletop. Customers and bank staff sit across from each other and move through the digital content by touching and swiping the screen.

> **A MOCK BRANCH allows new thinking to be tested in a risk-free environment.**

While novel technology has undoubtedly contributed to the buzz around the new store designs and facilitated an increase in sales, the Barclays team are convinced that people and process remain at the core of their transformation of the retail network. "Having the right people, with the right training and using the right systems and technology to facilitate a great customer experience is at the heart of our success," says Mike Amato.

The project to transform the branch network was less about the physical appearance of the branches, and more about changing the culture of the bank. The use of technology in the new environment has facilitated higher-quality and easier interaction between the staff and the customers, putting good old-fashioned service back at the heart of their customer relationships, and in the process making branches a better place to do business.

As the example shows, a mock branch allows new thinking to be tested in a risk-free environment. Mock branches may not be a new idea but the way they are being used has been updated. In the past, senior management and designers would have used these facilities to flesh out their thinking. Now, in a more inclusive approach to design, both staff and customers are invited to test-run new ideas at conception stage.

Queue Management has moved centre-stage in these projects, helping to deliver better customer service and greater efficiency.

A clear strategy for the customer's journey through the branch – arrival and check-in, management of waiting time, the service process, wrap-up and feedback at the end – provides a sound basis for delivering these. I have routinely observed a large number of banks branches. You can see the strategy behind the ones that work. They have been designed with the customer in mind.

MY FANTASY BANK BRANCH

Here's what I would see in my fantasy branch:

The view from the street is on-brand and unfussy; it strikes the right balance between promotional messages and visibility into the interior.

On entering the branch, a customer can quickly assimilate where he needs to go for what purpose. The branch is uncluttered – less is more when it comes to messages in banking halls. Way-finding signs and instructions are written in simple language rather than banking jargon.

The three types of visit are recognised: simple (transactional), inter-mediate (query) and complex (sales). It is also understood that not all customers will be served as soon as they walk through the door.

Options for accessing service are clearly defined, together with a well-designed check-in process, possibly supported by a member of staff to greet and assist. The greeter's purpose is to triage the customer's needs, and agree with the customer how and when they will access service.

Waiting time is actively managed. Opportunities are taken for relevant distraction. At the linear queue, the Call Forward System shows the right mix of digital content, to inform, amuse and entertain customers, distracting them from their waiting time. Longer waits to access complex service are hence made more tolerable.

A receipted service promise lets customers know how long they are going to wait; the bank's systems ensure that staff intervene if conditions change in a way that would prevent the promise from being kept.

Customers arriving for appointments have a check-in process as well, and the bank has optimised the balance between resource allocated to walk-ins and pre-booked appointments, to actively manage no-shows as well as people who arrive late or early.

Inter-branch expertise is harnessed through skills-based routing. Staff are not waiting idly for customers to arrive at their branch; they are available to talk to customers on the phone, routed from the call centre, or to conduct virtual meetings with customers in other branches, via a video link.

The atmosphere in the branch is calm and stress-free. There are no TV channels showing plane crashes and stock-market dives or radio stations playing competitors' ads.

Staff are also unstressed; they have the time to give good service – making eye contact, asking questions and waiting for the answers.

Technology is in use but not overt. A state-of-the-art footfall monitor system operates through digital cameras in the ceiling, tracking individuals around the branch to see where they dwell and, just as important, where they don't. This system is used alongside data from the queue management systems to understand the customer flow through the branch, to both update the staff-hours scheduling system for future days and help staff respond to current changes in demand levels, quickly and appropriately. It also shows the marketing department how many people are responding to the in-store displays and which areas of the store represent dead space.

THE FUTURE IS COMING

The majority of today's bank branches still exhibit the problems that most consumers would recognise. The research speaks for itself:

- Currently over 25% of customers of UK banks experience "unacceptable" delays in counter queues.[11]
- One major European bank estimates that a 5% improvement in customer satisfaction translates to a 2.4% increase in revenues due to lower attrition and additional sales.[12]
- Moving from low to high levels of customer satisfaction with branch service will be rewarded with a 45% fall in customer defection rates, a 26% increase in customer cross-buying and a 40% better referral rate.[13]

In recent years the banking industry is starting to take a new, more collaborative approach to innovation, directly engaging with experts and working with specialist suppliers to consider ways to reduce operating costs and improve the experience of the customers dealing with them.

The central plank of such activity is and must remain the IT infrastructure which is at the core of the data-hungry world that the banks must operate in. This, together with the need for strict compliance governs the backdrop to any changes and improvements that they can make to their branch infrastructure.

The branch is firmly at the centre of the industry's thinking as to how to successfully engage with customers, while leading industry suppliers, like Cisco Systems, are leading the way in creating IT strategies that are capable of transforming the bank's infrastructure and enabling seamless multi-channel interaction with the bank's customers.

The industry has two goals firmly in its sights – improve customer service and reduce operating costs – both of which will benefit their customers in the long term.

14

BUILDING A
BUZZ

THE NATURE OF GROWTH

"The idea that companies progress smoothly from acorns into oak trees is just a load of tosh. They grow from acorns into motorbikes, motorbikes into gorillas and then gorillas into blocks of flats."

I was sitting with David Singleton, then deputy managing director of Lloyds TSB Middle Market Division. The bank had been carrying out research into the nature of growth in medium-sized businesses and he was sharing the top-line findings with me.

"At the end of each run of growth they will come up against fundamental choices about how to move forward. A crossroads."

While we were building the queueing business in the mid-90s I was offered the opportunity to work part-time within the UK government's Innovation Unit. The Unit was tasked with promoting enterprise and innovation across the UK economy and my particular role within this was to work with the marketing community, addressing the needs of small and medium enterprises. It was a great opportunity not only to contribute to a fantastic marketing challenge but also a chance to rub shoulders with business leaders, industrialists and academics, and get access to their ideas and experience. It gave me fascinating insight into a wealth of knowledge about managing growth.

I was able to carry back what I learned into Qm.

There were three distinct phases in developing our business before it became part of Qmatic Group. Each one was quite different in character and called for revised priorities and skill sets to be applied in order to create and sustain success:

Phase One

Our kick-off stage, this phase was about harnessing available technology to solve a problem we perceived in everyday life – that of making linear queues work better. Bringing our customer, Post Office, into the dialogue early reduced risk in our investment and speeded the arrival of revenue. At this stage our business consisted of a small project team working up an idea, sustained by little more than enthusiasm, the goodwill of key stakeholders and a healthy dose of part-time perspiration.

Phase Two

This phase had us building a sustainable business model while creating a market space for our new products. Our small but loyal band had to grasp the nettle of becoming a management team as new recruits were hired to service the growing needs of our customers. Our company invented, manufactured, installed and maintained complex electronic systems in clients' premises and set a standard that put larger, more established businesses to shame.

OUR SMALL BUT LOYAL TEAM had to grasp the nettle of becoming a management team as new recruits were hired.

Creating the market for queue management in the UK required

tenacity, commitment and research. The knowledge that we compiled, which became our "art and science," drove value-creation in the business, setting the shape of our product development and the tone of our communications with clients and prospects. We fought for growth and we succeeded. It wasn't all one way though. During this phase we made an acquisition and overstretched ourselves, and had to endure a painful period of consolidation. After this we added fresh talent to the management team and found ourselves reinvigorated, creating dramatic growth once again.

Phase Three

Selling the company to the management team, was a watershed and a huge learning experience. It forced the founders of the business to step out of the role of executive responsibility and to become mentors, passing their experience and knowledge to the new team who took over the challenge of successfully growing the business and our profit. It was a time for reflection and a chance to change gear. And it was scary to let go and trust the guys to do a great job even though they were hugely talented – like letting your teenage son drive your brand-new company car – would it come back in one piece? There is no doubt that the addition of a new CEO and CFO during this phase made a significant difference to our confidence levels and to the company's performance.

> **IT WAS SCARY to let go – like letting your teenage son drive your brand-new company car.**

THE ALCHEMY OF SUCCESS

We had kicked off Qm in the mid-90s, and in 2004 the owners sold it to the management team in a "vendor-initiated management buyout" (VIMBO) backed by London-based venture capitalists, Advantage Capital. In 2007 the opportunity arose to sell again, generating a five-times investment multiple for Advantage's fund in just 30 months. The second sale was to Nordic-based Altor Equity Partners, who pulled off a strategic coup by buying both Qm and Qmatic, creating an enterprise with the merged firms' combined knowledge, experience, product base, and global reach.

For me, this current phase is, if anything, the most exciting. We have long since proven that queue management delivers value to our clients' organisations, and our regular customers around the globe are gaining massive competitive advantage from our knowledge and solutions. Qmatic Group is well-positioned to capitalise on the next phase of market adoption of Customer Flow Management, the best practice of queue management.

Sustaining successful organisations as they form, grow and reach out for their potential is a journey not a destination. And whatever your business, the competition are ever present, trying to win customer preference away from you.

In considering the drivers for and blockers of growth, it's easy to ignore the basics. Back in my Innovation Unit days I chaired a number of dinners for middle-market business leaders around the UK entitled "Let's Talk Business," sponsored by the government, Lloyds Bank and the Chartered Institute of Marketing, in which we asked attendees to debate what they found most challenging about running their businesses. In every

195

session I heard "time management, prioritisation and delegation" at the top of the list of issues that business leaders and their teams struggled with in their quest for making a better enterprise. While other problems and opportunities were debated, some with a regional twist, these fundamental tasks of management were always in the top five. In reality, if your team are not capable of organising their own time effectively, delegating tasks and delivering against the goals you set, then success will always elude you.

No one wants to fail, but the culture, climate and structure within the business may not enable them to do excellent work. If your staff are fire-fighting problems caused by "wrong first time" quality and wobbly processes, then they will always be "too busy" when it comes to contributing their insight – the vital spark that improves everyone's role, attitude and performance.

Breaking out of these negative behaviours is difficult and requires determination to bring about improvement and make it stick.

WINNING

One of the big triumphs of the Innovation Unit was a document entitled "Winning." It became one of the most requested business publications the government had ever put its name to. "Winning" was researched through interviews with 100 of the best-performing organisations in the UK – not all of which were commercial enterprises. The interview analysis was conducted with the help of the University of Warwick and published with the support of CBI (the Confederation of British Industry). The lessons contained within it are as fresh and relevant today as when they were first written in 1995.

This was the opening paragraph:

"You feel it the moment you enter a competitive company; there is a buzz that suggests confidence and success. But how is this buzz achieved? What are the key factors and how can these be emulated in all British companies? This study of over 100 of the Best Companies has shown that winning UK-based companies share a number of characteristics. It does not matter whether those companies are in the service or manufacturing sector; the key elements contributing to their success are the same; importantly, they focus on three core issues: champions of change, employees and customers. These key success factors are not in themselves new but they do reinforce previous messages. Nine out of ten of the companies interviewed exhibit "ingredients for success"; it is no accident that these are all "people related" and fundamental to the adoption and evolution of best practices. As one managing director observed: "Excellent companies know people make the difference!"

Ingredients found in UK's 100 best companies

A. Winning companies are led by visionary, enthusiastic champions who
- Have a vision that is owned throughout the organisation;
- Build demanding but realistic targets into the business strategy;
- Champion change, lead by example, and accept managed risk;

- Generate an open, communicative management style throughout the organisation;
- Focus on their customers.

B. Winning companies know their customers; they
- Know and anticipate the future needs of their customers;
- Have a realistic understanding of their competitors and how to beat them in competition for the customers;
- Know the drivers in their market;
- Focus on the customer and cultivate an active partnership towards total customer satisfaction;
- Collaborate with customers, other companies, suppliers and academia to maximise capabilities and minimise risk.

C. Winning companies unlock the potential of their people; they
- Empower all employees by creating individual ownership and focus on customers;
- Simplify the internal systems wherever possible;
- Clearly communicate company performance;
- Encourage a team approach;
- Train at all levels – professional development, multi-skilling, updating;
- Measure and benchmark performance against direct competitors and other companies in other sectors;
- Install information and financial systems focussed on rapid provision of customer-relevant data.

D. Winning companies deliver products and services that exceed their customer expectations; they

- Adopt a philosophy of total quality in all company behaviour that emphasises delighting the customers with all aspects of the product and services;
- Measure customer perceptions of products and service;
- Deliver continuous improvements in all value-added aspects;
- Seek to continuously reduce customer costs;
- Develop partnerships with their suppliers.

E. Winning companies continuously introduce differentiated products and services; they

- Actively develop their future product and service offer even though today's is still a success;
- Exploit new technology or legislation to drive new product innovation;
- Customise the product and service;
- Radically improve speed to market;
- Adopt multi-functional teams to drive innovations forward.

This is powerful stuff. Don't just skim over the words on the page. Take a little time to consider them and their meaning and how they apply to your organisation. Table a meeting to discuss the checklist with your colleagues. To what extent do the behaviours described above reflect the actions and values of you and your colleagues? Can you truly describe yourselves as being driven by your customers' perceived needs? Do you have enthusiastic champions of change sharing a clear vision of success?

If you don't like your answers then it's down to you to change it.

I have successfully used the Winning Checklist to drive change and measure its adoption. Simply turn it into a score sheet and get all of your team to score their collective behaviours every month – every line, out of ten. The items with the biggest variation in scores across your group will tell you where the biggest opportunities for improvement lie.

SPELL SUCCESS WITH THREE Ps

If you want to change your organisation into a winning one, and make your business buzz, there are three words that you must remember. Strangely they all begin with P.

Passion

Passion is the most important P. In my experience it provides the motivation and the self-belief to get things done. And it's infectious. Watch people who talk about things that they passionately believe in – it's illuminating. Instead of asking people what they do at those social gatherings, try asking "What's your passion?" For most people, it's their

> **INSTEAD OF asking people what they do at social gatherings, try asking, "What's your passion?"**

hobbies or their children rather than their work. If you can get people that passionate about what you do then you will change opinions.

It's not as hard as it sounds. First you have to believe it. Make sure that you understand what you are talking about and find firm evidence to support what you say. Don't be frightened to be controversial, but be prepared to back up your passion with facts.

Passion makes your business culture sizzle. It allows people to stop saying "I can't" and to find ways how they can. And it will differentiate your sales people from the bored, uncommitted competitors who turn up at their prospect's office with a brochure and a false smile.

In the case of Qm and Qmatic, creating our knowledge base has been key to generating and sustaining the passion around what we do. The five headings under "Know their customers" in the checklist above are precisely the questions that we have continued to target in developing our business proposition; they reflect our behaviour in partnering customers and suppliers when developing a new proposition.

People

The checklist provides five headings under "Unlock the potential of their people," all of which are vital to creating and sustaining a winning enterprise. In my experience it is essential to consider the people who work for your customers and your suppliers too – effectively your whole value chain. The interdependence of each party needs to be recognised and communicated and each member of the extended team should understand his or her role within it. This can sometimes be difficult when your customer has a million things to do other than deal with your particular

> **YOU HAVE TO work with people and through people.**

issue. We have found this many times in the queueing industry. No one is called "Queue Manager" among our customers; responsibility for access to service in branches usually falls in with other significant tasks and so it has proven essential to move queueing up the priority list by focussing on the real business benefits that we can create when we can truly engage with a client organisation.

You have to work with people and through people. The ability to build a personal network has never been more important if you want to succeed in business. You need to be able to motivate people to buy into your ideas and persuade them to act on them. Interpersonal skills across a variety of media – telephone, text, email, letter, Skype, face to face – are vital to this. You must be compelling in all of them. Develop your own style but seek feedback to make sure that you are getting across what you want to say and confirm that it's having the desired impact on your audience.

Dare to be different. I have found that introducing myself at a senior level to a new client using "snail mail" can be very effective. Letters are almost a novelty these days and provided that your message is short and exactly relevant it will be seen and get you noticed.

I found a very effective way to differentiate myself when presenting to a new client. I ditched the laptop, the product brochures and price lists, and relied on conversation. I realised that this approach had a number of advantages. With no electronic props I was completely

I DITCHED the laptop, product brochures, price lists...

in control of my delivery – no buttons to push or screens to freeze. I could keep eye contact with my prospects and watch their body language as

I presented. I couldn't be lazy; I needed to think through and rehearse exactly where I wanted the conversation to go, what I was going to say and how I would back it up to ensure that I was word-perfect on the day. I would make sure that I created the right "leave-behind paper" – a short, punchy document summarising the key points of my presentation and evidence, along with a brief introduction to my company. This would allow my prospect to reflect accurately on the conver-

> I WOULD REVEAL this document at the end of the meeting, or better still, provide a link to a special page.

sation that we had had, and to pass it on to colleagues – effectively becoming my communication channel into the organisation. I would reveal this document at the end of the meeting or, better still, provide a link to a special page on our website that informed me every time my prospect or their colleagues accessed it.

People are your business. You know that. Empower them. Make them feel like they are part of a special team and that they as individuals are important. Respect them, listen to them, talk to them (never at them). Practice two-way feedback.

Process

The last two headings of the checklist define areas of "Process." Exceeding customer expectations and continuously introducing differentiated products and services will help you to retain customer preference in the face of competition. This behaviour will also help to manage the need to discount your offer.

Innovation is the lifeblood of this process. I described earlier what I called task-centric innovation, a no-nonsense approach to focussing your efforts precisely on a specific opportunity based out of a clearly defined customer need. In our case, our very first product was derived this way and it became our standard way of developing a new product or improving an existing one.

The two processes that have driven more value than any others in our business are those for product development and structured selling. The first one created our value proposition, the second our revenue and margin.

I believe that any outcome is the consequence of the process that created it – whether you designed the process or not, a series of events took place that gave rise to an output. If you didn't like the result then the wrong process created it. It follows that if you want a specific result you need to create the perfect process that will guarantee its delivery. The better we prepare the process the more risk we remove from the outcome. Measurement and continuous improvement are key.

This was the essential belief behind the structured sales process that we created, which we dubbed "Stepchange."

STEPCHANGE: STRUCTURED SELLING

In selling to our clients I have averaged a near-100% success rate. It's not because I am a fabulous salesman with a huge personality; it's because I follow a process that works. Let me try to give you some insight into that process.

1. What's your offer?

You need to be very clear about what you can offer the client. What are the products and services that you have available to sell? A salesman who always comes back with an order for something you haven't got and can't make isn't a salesman – he's an order-taker. He has applied no skill to the process of matching up prospects with what your business can do; he has simply held a meeting, listened to what the client has said they want and offered to supply it. That's just not good enough. Whoever goes and sits in front of the client needs to understand the rules before they leave their base office. What products are currently available for sale? Does your company have the ability to customise, and if so what are the lead times and associated costs? Are you able to develop a tailored product to meet a specific need, and if so what is the process by which you engage with a client to do this?

> A SALESMAN WHO always comes back with an order for something you haven't got and can't make isn't a salesman – he's an order-taker.

Even though a prospect might be sold on a particular way of solving a problem, that doesn't make it necessarily the only or the best way to bring about an improvement. The salesman has a duty of care to assist the client to come to a considered view about all of the options available and to make an informed choice. To do this the salesman must comprehend the issues that the client faces in detail and be able to articulate the ways in which his proposed solution adds value.

Bullshit just won't do it. Knowledge is required.

2. Turning suspects...

A great place for a new sales person to start out is with their organisation's existing customers. Gaining a thorough understanding of how the products get used and what benefits can be derived will provide substance to their case-study presentations and create confidence. They will be able to deliver their evidence with conviction if they have stared into the whites of an existing customer's eyes and heard his views with their own ears.

From here it's a relatively straightforward process to consider how other organisations might benefit from the solutions you have available.

In the early days of Qm, with our "Cashier Number Three Please" product, it wasn't rocket science to consider the banks with their linear queues as potential targets for what we did. I simply drew up a list of all of the UK banks and compiled useful information like how many branches they had, where their head office was, where their purchasing people were based and how their operational departments were structured. This gave me a sense of the scale of opportunity with each target and how many people I would need to persuade.

3. ...into prospects

Continuing the desk research it is important to get a sense of the style and culture of the organisation. Most organisations develop their own linguistic style, their own way of talking about the challenges that they face. It's important to assimilate this in preparation for your meeting. It will allow you to express yourself in their terms. And what do

> **ORGANISATIONS DEVELOP their own linguistic style.**

the press say about them? Is there anything relevant mentioned in their annual report or the chairman's address to the annual general shareholders' meeting? All these clues can help you to build an identikit picture of the organisation you are targeting and determine whether you believe they will buy into what you have to offer.

4. Walk the store

For me, walking the store was the acid test. This was my chance to examine the way they currently did things and to consider how, if at all, the products, services and knowledge that I had available could add value to their business and their customers' lives. It also provided me with more anecdotal evidence that I could use as part of my initial pitch to the client. I was experiencing what it was

FRONT-LINE STAFF in the stores are a great source of information.

like to be a customer in their stores. Were there any missed opportunities to improve the customer experience or to raise efficiency? To increase sales? Front-line staff in the stores were also a great source of information, not only about issues within the customer experience but also with ideas about who to contact within their organisation.

5. Prepare your case

By Stage 4 I had parked a number of suspects for later consideration and would now be down to a hardcore list of qualified prospects, whom I believed had a need that I could meet and an opportunity large enough to justify me investing the time to try to make a sale. At this stage I was able to create a rough "return on investment" model to help me understand the size of investment I would expect the prospect to make and the win they could expect in return. This gave me the confidence to continue the approach.

In our case the sales cycle can be quite long – certainly measured in months – and so it was important to create a pipeline of opportunity where I could spread the workload in order to make it more manageable and attempt to deliver a steady stream of revenue potential.

I would make my first targets those organisations that had everything to play for – maybe the number two in the market segment who was ambitious to be number one, or an organisation that used to be a major player but needed to make up lost ground. In some cases it was as simple as those companies who consistently demonstrated a track record in innovation and customer service.

6. First contact

Having selected my victim it was necessary to consider the most effective way of making contact with the decision-makers in the business. It's important that initial contact is made at executive level, and the sales proposition is expressed in a way that fits in with the target customer's current thinking. Initially I would seek mutual contacts to make an introduction, but in the absence of that my favoured approach has been a very short letter, no more than two lines. The letter needs to deliver a compelling message but not a complete

> **MY FAVOURED APPROACH has been a very short letter, no more than two lines.**

answer. For example, in the past I have written to the chief executive of a retailer complimenting them on a new store format and suggesting ways in which it could be improved further while asking for a referral to the relevant party within the prospect's organisation. It's then a question of chasing, normally with the CEO's personal assistant, to gain traction for this message. Patience is a necessity; losing your temper and expressing your frustration when you have to email yet another copy of what you sent just won't cut it. It has taken me as long as five months to get through this stage.

7. First meeting

Gaining a first meeting is a key milestone. It needs to be prepared for with the utmost care. By the time that you walk through the door you need to be thoroughly rehearsed in what you plan to say. You need to have a clear goal for this meeting – what outcome should a successful meeting produce? You also need to have considered the questions they may ask or the objections they may raise and how you will respond to keep your agenda on course. In my experience this is not a good time to extemporise, particularly if you are unsure of your ground. If you

> **USE THE FIRST MEETING** to begin establishing trust and credibility. Be prepared to give before you receive.

don't know the answer, say so, but then make sure you find out and report back. Use this first meeting to begin establishing trust and credibility. Be prepared to give before you receive.

8. Permission audit

Typically, for me, my call to action for the first meeting has been to seek a prospect's permission to go into store and confirm my preliminary findings around the value that I believe that I can add by applying appropriate queue management techniques. This stage may also involve hosting a Retail Safari for a group of the client's senior employees so that they experience for themselves the view that I take of their operations.

Whatever equivalent call to action you have from the first meeting you should now view your contact with the client as a series of steps that ultimately lead you to closing your sale. This is a measurable process that allows you to build and manage a pipeline of sales prospects.

9. Proposal & confirmation

By the time I reached the proposal stage there was a measure of trust in the client's mind concerning our knowledge and credentials. Store visits had provided feedback as to the kind of value that we expected to generate by applying formal queue management techniques. It was now time to test the client's belief in the proposition by asking for action and funding.

The client should now be able to formally commit to the trial process. In advance of the trial it's important for both parties to agree on the criteria for a successful outcome so that everyone is completely clear as to what they are trying to achieve.

10. Trial

The trial is more than a test of the product itself, it's a chance for the customer to experience all aspects of the service that you offer prior to making a major financial commitment. If your service is sub-optimal the client can walk away without significant financial penalty.

Your whole team needs to be fully briefed and aware of the risks and opportunities involved in each client trial. It is essential that the client receives the best service and support levels that you can offer if the trial is to lead to a successful outcome.

For us, it was essential that the client's staff were thoroughly trained, confident and comfortable in using our system. My biggest fear for any business is when people having bought your solution stop seeing the value of using it, usually through ignorance of how it works. This is more threatening than any conventional competition. This destroys markets.

> **THIS IS MORE THREATENING than any conventional competition. This destroys markets.**

11. Business case

One of the great things about trials is that while you are validating the efficacy of the solution, you are able to observe first-hand how and by how much they add value to your customer's business. It's only when you fully understand the value that you deliver to your customers – in their terms not yours – that you can fully appreciate how to price the supply of that solution in an equitable way. Sometimes the system doesn't get used the way you expect or additional benefits might come out that you hadn't thought of. When we first put Call Forward into one American retailer they told us that in addition to the customer experience and productivity gains that we predicted, they also experienced a reduction in "sweet hearting" – the collusion between staff and customer in not scanning some items – because the linear queue randomised which customer was served by which member of staff.

12. Asking for the order

When you go to a fine restaurant, when do they give you the bill? Do they rush out halfway through the starter and plonk it on the table? Or do they wait until they have delivered their best shot – the whole meal, and with their best service, when you are replete – and then, and only then, say, "Was everything to your satisfaction, sir, madam?" and present you with the bill?

If you present your bill too early you make it much harder to demonstrate the value the client is paying for. If you time it right, so that the client perceives that value, it's much easier to charge what you think is appropriate and secure the order.

13. Retain

Servicing existing clients is much cheaper and easier than constantly finding new ones. If you look after them well, they will trust you to keep delivering value to their business. Offer advice and insight. Keep them passionate about the solution. Give your champion small wins that they can bank while you build towards the further close that you want to achieve. Be patient but be focussed. Plan every meeting and every stage so that the results become inevitable.

> **GIVE YOUR CHAMPION small wins they can bank.**

HOW MUCH SUCCESS CAN YOU HANDLE?

In my experience, the combined effect of the 3 Ps, Passion, People and Process, transform businesses into customer-focussed, success-hungry deliverers of change. If you truly want your business to buzz, I don't know a better way than this to get you there.

To me, the right people, managed appropriately and working within the right set of processes, will deliver a consistent, quality result which automatically adjusts for risk in the environment. Passion is the vital spark. It's the spice that delivers an extra zing, making it fun for your people and special for your customers. Never lose your passion.

AFTERWORD

WHEN THE IDEA OF WRITING THIS BOOK was first discussed, the prospect terrified me. How could I possibly fill a whole volume with words about queueing? I guess it's amazing how much you learn about a subject when you live it, think about it, and work on it pretty much every day of your life for nearly twenty years. I also realised that many people have found what I have to say about it interesting – that or they were just being extremely polite.

Queueing continues to be a tremendously rewarding business to be in. I have met some fabulous people over the years and many clients have become friends in the process. And because people get passionate about delivering great service they get caught up with the idea of proactive queue management and how that can transform customer experience and operational efficiency.

Queues are a great leveller. There are very few of us for whom the word and the practice have no meaning. But there are some.

In late 2008 I was excited to receive an invitation to a dinner given by the Royal Society for the encouragement of Arts, Manufactures and Commerce, at Buckingham Palace. The society, a charitable body, exists to promote human progress through the efforts of its 27,000 strong fellowship. The dinner was, I believe, being held to celebrate 200 years of royal patronage.

The RSA's president, HRH Prince Philip, was to be in attendance, creating a very special occasion for all invited. The dinner would take place in the Ballroom – the same room in which investitures are held – and would be preceded by drinks in the Long Gallery.

When the date finally arrived, it was a seasonally cold and frosty mid-December evening. The streets of Central London were decorated with Christmas lights, and all of the stores with their seasonal displays just added to the atmosphere of anticipation. As I arrived at the palace with the other guests, our invitation cards were scrutinised by the policemen on gate duty and we walked the short distance across the crisp, crunchy courtyard and into the palace where a huge Christmas tree, decorated with silver and gold crowns, was proudly displayed. With our coats removed we made our way up to the splendid, high-ceilinged Long Gallery and, with champagne in hand, were soon mingling and chatting among ourselves.

At the appointed hour, Prince Philip made his entrance. He was escorted through the room, stopping to chat with some of the guests along the way. I looked on while continuing to make small talk with those around me. With a flash of surprise I suddenly realised that HRH was at my elbow and was talking to me.

"So, young man, what do you do?"

I gulped a couple of times and said "Good evening, sir," and then auto-pilot took over and before I knew it, I was into my standard introduction routine. "Sir, imagine yourself standing in line at the post office," I said. "It's my voice that says "Cashier Number Three Please!" I then looked in horror at the perplexed face of His Royal Highness as I realised that what I had just said was completely outside of his personal experience!

THERE IS NO DOUBT IN MY MIND that for the vast majority of us the mathematics and psychology of queueing will continue to have a massive impact on our lives in the years to come. This book has discussed the principles that govern the way waiting works and used the areas of banking and retail to illustrate the difference that can be created when some intelligent thinking and a hefty dose of common sense is applied. The same ideas are equally applicable to other areas of our lives – healthcare, government, travel and leisure. It's all about giving customers access to service in the most efficient and effective way possible, eliminating unnecessary waits and making those that remain as productive as possible.

And it doesn't stop there. Queues and queue management exist in all aspects of our lives, whether it's aircraft coming in to land, traffic jams on major roads, crowds at concerts, the way our phone calls are handled by call centres or the software that allows our personal computers to manage the simultaneous multiple requests that we make of them.

Waiting is all around us, in everything we do. Let's work together to make it better.

ACKNOWLEDGEMENTS

I COULDN'T COMPLETE THIS BOOK without acknowledging the energy, commitment and perspiration of the whole team that worked with us at Qm and now as Qmatic, and that includes not just the people who are or have been on the official payroll but all of our friends, supporters, suppliers and customers who "caught the bug" and made what we have achieved so far possible. There are so many examples of personal heroism from the team that I could fill another book with their stories, but can I just say a humble "Thank you, you were magnificent!" to each and every one of you.

In the customer camp, I should particularly like to mention Jo Moran and the team at Marks & Spencer from whom I have learned so much about delivering excellent customer service in retailing; Richard Johns at Argos who educated me about retail operations; Richard Newland and Damian Wild at HSBC, and Nic Parmaksizian and Mike Amato at Barclays, who made me believe that banks could change; and Cameron MacQuarrie at Cisco for his tireless support. And of course special thanks must go to the Post Office, who gave us our break, particularly to Ian Oakley and Richard Lock.

I would also like to thank Paco Underhill for being a tireless inspiration; David Maister for eloquently putting into words so much of what I feel about delivering great service; and Professor Richard "Dick" Larson, who not only encouraged me to write this but went to the trouble of picking me up on my spelling. In reviewing the text for this book Dick reminded me of the correct spelling for "queueing." This is not the first time this has come up. Interestingly I always used to spell it "queueing" but bowed my head to use "queuing," believing it to be a more internationally acceptable form of the word (certainly Microsoft's spell-check thinks so!). I promised Dick that I would mention his chastisement of me.

I am of course indebted to the team at Qmatic for allowing me access to and use of their case-study and archive material in the compilation of this book.

I would also like to offer my heartfelt gratitude to Martin Liu at Marshall Cavendish and to Alistair Agnew at Qmatic for having faith in my ability to write and for backing this enterprise; and a massive thank you to Justin Lau, who as editor was challenged with the unspeakable task of turning my words into the book you see before you.

And finally I must thank those of my friends, family and colleagues who have tirelessly supported me in the drafting of this manuscript and patiently read and offered feedback at each stage.

NOTES

1. Robert F. Cope III, Rachelle F. Cope & Harold E. Davis, "Disney's Virtual Queues: A Strategic Opportunity to Co-Brand Services?" *Journal of Business & Economic Research* (October 2008).

2. Richard C. Larson, "Perspectives on Queues: Social Justice and the Psychology of Queueing," *Operations Research* (November/ December 1987).

3. David Maister, "The Psychology of Waiting Lines" (1985). www.davidmaister.com

4. Larson, *op cit.*

5. Datamonitor, "Business Trends: European Banking Technology" (2007).

6. Edward Anderson, "A Note on Managing Waiting Lines," UT McCombs School of Business (2003).

7. Cisco IBSG, "The New Key to Retail Success" (August 2008).

8. Nick Bidmead, Georges Massoud, & Piotr Romanowski, "Bank branches that meet customer needs," *McKinsey Quarterly Journal* (August 2007).

9. Patrick Hennessy & Melinda Kite, "Missed appointments cost NHS £575m a year," *Sunday Telegraph* (23 August 2005).

10. Kate Devlin, "Missed hospital appointments 'costing NHS £600m,'" *Telegraph* (12 August 2009).

11. GfK NOP Tracker (2005).

12. Cisco IBSG client experience quoted March 2006.

13. EFMA/Finalta, "Improving Branch Service: A Priority for Change" (March 2005).

RECOMMENDED READING

Damian Barr "The Waiting Game: Are We Losing the Knack?" *The Times* (28 November 2009).

Edward de Bono, *The Mechanism of Mind* (New York: Simon & Schuster, 1969).

Marc Beaujean, Vincent Cremers, & Francisco Pedro Goncalves Pereira, "How Europe's Banks Can Profit From Loyal Customers," *McKinsey Quarterly* web exclusive (November 2005).

Marc Beaujean, Jonathan Davidson, & Stacey Madge, "The Moment of Truth in Customer Service," *McKinsey Quarterly* (February 2006).

Datamonitor, "Branch Strategies for the 21st Century in European Retail Banking (Strategic Focus)" (September 2008).

K. Katz, B. Larson, & R. Larson, "Prescription for the Waiting-in-Line Blues: Entertain, Enlighten and Engage," *Sloan Management Review* (Winter 1991).

Richard C. Larson, "The Queue Inference Engine," *Management Science* (May 1990).

Michael Sisk, "The Future of the Bank Branch," Bank Technology News (July 2009).